The Way *through* the Wilderness

One Woman's Spiritual Journey

*Behold, I will do a new thing;
now it shall spring forth; shall
ye not know it? I will even make a
way in the wilderness, and
rivers in the desert.
Isaiah 43:18–19*

BY
MERYL JAMES-SEBRO, PH.D.

World rights reserved. This book or any portion thereof may not be copied or reproduced in any form or manner whatever, except as provided by law, without the written permission of the publisher, except by a reviewer who may quote brief passages in a review.

The author assumes full responsibility for the accuracy of all facts and quotations as cited in this book. The opinions and viewpoints expressed in this book are the author's personal views and interpretations, based upon her life experiences and education, and do not necessarily reflect those of the publisher.

This book is provided with the understanding that the publisher is not engaged in giving spiritual, legal, medical, or other professional advice. If authoritative advice is needed, the reader should seek the counsel of a competent professional.

Copyright © 2025 Meryl James-Sebro, Ph.D.
Copyright © 2025 TEACH Services, Inc.
Published in Calhoun, Georgia, USA
ISBN-13: 978-1-4796-1811-8 (Paperback)
ISBN-13: 978-1-4796-1823-1 (ePub)
Library of Congress Control Number: 2025911391

All Scripture quotations, unless otherwise indicated, are taken from the King James Version®. Public domain.

Scripture quotations marked MSG are taken from The Message, copyright © 1993, 2002, 2018 by Eugene H. Peterson. Used by permission of NavPress. All rights reserved. Represented by Tyndale House Publishers, Inc.

Scripture quotations marked NKJV are taken from the New King James Version®. Copyright © 1990 by Thomas Nelson. Used by permission. All rights reserved.

Scripture quotations marked ESV are taken from the English Standard Version. Copyright © 2001 by Crossway, a publishing ministry of Good News Publishers. Used by permission. All rights reserved.

Scripture quotations marked NIV are taken from the New International Version. Copyright © 1973, 1978, 1984, 2011 by Biblica, Inc®. Used by permission. All rights reserved worldwide.

Published by

TEACH Services, Inc.
PUBLISHING
www.TEACHServices.com • (800) 367-1844

Praise for Meryl James-Sebro's
The Way through the Wilderness

The Way through the Wilderness is written in a clear, accessible, and captivating style, informed by an impressively wide range of personal and Biblical narratives that illustrate the blessings and benefits of one woman's spiritual journey.

This beautifully written book shines a new and creative light on our understanding of the wilderness as a place of hope and new beginnings. It is a book that everyone should read.

Walter Douglas, Ph.D., Professor Emeritus & Chair
Dept. of History and Philosophy of World Religion, Andrews University,
Michigan, USA

In *The Way through the Wilderness*, Dr. Meryl James-Sebro takes her readers on a soul-stirring exploration and transformative spiritual journey through the wilderness of life.

With profound and scholarly insights, vulnerability, and a deep connection to her heritage, she charts a path forward in the search for purpose and a deeper meaning of life, questioning long-held traditions and opinions.

Marshalling her own experiences, she makes the point that wildernesses will be successfully navigated, not in one's physical strength or religious observances, but in relationship with the triune God.

Join James-Sebro on this fresh and enlightening journey to uncover the sacred paths to the true source of empowerment, wholeness, and real fulfillment.

Lola Alakija, Pastor & Broadcast Journalist
Lagos, Nigeria

This spiritual autobiography by Dr. Meryl James-Sebro is an extraordinary, intimate, passionate, and introspective journey, one woman's attempt to discover meaning and purpose in her life.

She takes us on a spiritual odyssey and faith pilgrimage, traversing America and the Caribbean over the last forty years of her life. It is a journey filled with notable highs and lows, but a story crafted with incredible grace and dignity. With candor and vulnerability, she weaves a deeply emotional memoir that brings tears to her readers but is also a source of encouragement and empowerment to those facing similar circumstances.

This beautifully written and skillfully crafted book captures Dr. James-Sebro's conviction that the way through the wilderness, no matter the kind of wilderness we find ourselves in, is possible only as we put our trust and confidence in a loving and merciful God.

Trevor O'Reggio, Ph.D., Chair & Professor

Church History Dept., Seventh-day Adventist Seminary,
Andrews University, Michigan, USA

Dedicated to my sister,

Beverly Melony Casimir James
1944 – 2023
HALLELUJAH!!!

CONTENTS

ACKNOWLEDGEMENTS		ix
PROLOGUE		xi
CHAPTER 1	A HAND OF GREEN FIGS	15
CHAPTER 2	CHURCH INITIATION	18
CHAPTER 3	FROM PLACE TO PURPOSE	22
CHAPTER 4	"SMALL CHURCH"	27
CHAPTER 5	THE JOURNEY NOW START	31
CHAPTER 6	THE NEARNESS OF GOD	39
CHAPTER 7	GROUND ZERO: FAITH AND FAVOUR VERSUS FEAR	45
CHAPTER 8	THE INSIDE ENEMY	54
CHAPTER 9	POWER IN THE BLOOD	59
CHAPTER 10	OUT-OF-PLACE WOMEN	65
CHAPTER 11	RECHARGE YOUR BATTERY	74
CHAPTER 12	SPIRT-FILLED AND FIRED UP	82
CHAPTER 13	LESSONS FROM MY GARDEN	88
CHAPTER 14	THE INSURRECTION VS. THE RESURRECTION	98
CHAPTER 15	ONE LITTLE LIGHT	104

CHAPTER 16	THE DIVINE CONNECTION	110
CHAPTER 17	LOVE IN THE TIME OF HATE	116
CHAPTER 18	THE WAY	120
CHAPTER 19	ANSWERING THE CALL	127
CHAPTER 20	FULL CIRCLE	134
BIBLIOGRAPHY		141

ACKNOWLEDGEMENTS

All thanks to the holy Trinity for the *chutzpah* to pen this journey. No matter how much one tries, in an effort like this, it is rare that one remembers every experience. I may well be guilty of misplacing one of the most important stories.

My nephew, perhaps no more than six at that time, had been spending the weekend with me. I explained that we were going to church and then to brunch. It was New York City, at the time when the literati, the glitterati, the newly born religiorati, and the otherati frequented major assemblies at one of the fanciest public spaces in mid-town Manhattan. A dear friend, one of the newly born religiorati, had invited me, and so Alaistair, dressed in his little white jeans and shirt, tagged along. To be truthful, it was an interesting and inspiring lecture-like presentation, not a sermon. On leaving the fancy building, my nephew asked, "Aunty, did you say we were going to church?"

"Yes, and now we're going to brunch," I replied cheerfully.

He looked up at me with wide-eyed innocence: "But they only said God once!"

Undoubtedly that was the biggest push to my spiritual journey. So, thank you, Alaistair, for leading me to the writing of this *oeuvre*.

I am grateful to my husband, Tony, whose love and great sensitivity provided time and space, kindly ignoring my unusually silent moments.

My only sister and sibling, Beverly, to whom this book has been dedicated, passed near the completion of the writing, but my love and gratitude for her support remain alive.

Catherine James-Bell (not related), the clerk of the Golden Gate All Nations Seventh-day Adventist Church in Naples, Florida, and Hidy Matthew, the leader of the Youth Department there, inspired some of the more "preachy" sections, through invitations to speak at our online Wednesday evening prayer meetings and Friday vesper sessions. Dr. Walter Douglas and Dr. Trevor O'Reggio were kind enough to read and greenlight the manuscript. They all have deepened my gratitude, respect, and admiration.

Special thanks to long-time sister-friends: Dr. Leola Weithers, Pastor Brenda Billingy, and Jennifer Martin in the US; Pastor Lola Alakija of Nigeria; and Dr. Margaret Gill of Barbados, and to a new Spirit-filled friend, Janeen Smith; they supported in ways beyond description. Thanks also to writer brother and knowledge-packed friend, Knolly Moses of Trinidad and Jamaica, for expert technical advice. Timothy Hullquist, Kathy Pflugrad, Vanessa Boeser (editor), Alyssa Newman (design and production director), and the team at TEACH Services have eased the challenges of the post-writing phase with their meticulous attention to detail, and for this I am especially grateful. Moreover, I extend my deep appreciation to everyone who, through these pages, is helped to discern and follow the guidance of the Holy Spirit *through* the wilderness. Stay blessed!

PROLOGUE

At a certain point in one's earthly existence, it is important to hit the pause button, to evaluate one's life and to chart a path forward. Mine happened in my early thirties. It became ever so clear that the vacuum I was feeling could not be filled by academic, emotional, professional, or financial success. Thus began an internal exploration that revealed a spiritual foundation with a force that had guided and protected me … even when I was not always aware of it. This, then, is the thesis of *The Way* **through** *the Wilderness* … **through** being the operative word. Our loving Father never gives up on us. He continues to seek after us, patiently waiting for our complete surrender.

My reading of the Bible through the eyes of a feminist forced a new understanding of not only the way in which God honoured women, but the role He has carved out especially for women. Institutionalised undermining of this role points clearly to the tricky plan of the enemy, and the way in which institutions—government and religious—have been co-opted to confuse and forge demonic plans against women in order to dilute and withhold their power and participation.

> *Indeed the journey never stops. It continues in the dash between life and death. And we—you and I—will be victorious*

The following pages contain a series of flashbacks and fast-forwards that have served as guidance. My own challenge has been to explore, in order to clarify, my own spirituality to help in the understanding of my responsibility as a woman of God in these perilous times when everyone—whether we acknowledge it or not—is being challenged to pick a side. Honesty and commitment to the revelation of the true self demand the need to speak up; speak out; interrupt; intervene and even interfere. Trouble the waters! Wave a flag!

What then does *The Way **through** the Wilderness* mean? Merging the spiritual, the intellectual, the physical, and the material—our sacred and secular lives—to find, understand, and activate purpose: true, divinely directed purpose. It is the search for purpose, in spite of pain. Hence the following flashbacks and fast-forwards explore and examine the route. Perhaps the most critical takeaway is the consistent need to **rewind**, **recall** and **reflect**. We will discover that:

1. God is real and alive;
2. His love is proactive;
3. His patience outwaits our running.

It is the only way to recognize, acknowledge, appreciate, and depend on God's goodness in our lives.

It has been a long and winding road, but in the words of Pastor Christopher Herbert, formerly known as the Trinbagonian calypsonian, "Tambu," "The Journey Now Start."

Indeed, the journey never stops. It continues in the dash between life and death. And we—you and I—will be victorious, as long as we follow His light that leads to that long and tortuous path ***through*** the wilderness. And if we can be the transmitter of His light in some small way, we are on the way to His way.

*** ***

Guidance Text:
"Behold, I will do a new thing; now it shall spring forth; shall ye not know it? I will even make a way in the wilderness, and rivers in the desert" (Isa. 43:19).

CHAPTER 1
A HAND OF GREEN FIGS

Wearing a long, white dress, a bunch of green figs—more commonly known as green bananas—in my hands and sitting in the yoga position before a life-sized photograph of an East Indian guru. That was my turning point, the pivotal moment that would turn, twist, twirl, and tantalise every thought, then toss me into an intense search for the Author of my being … the Soul of self … the Purpose for my living.

The journey may have begun long before that memorable afternoon in Port of Spain, Trinidad, but the recognised push had been a visit to a midtown Manhattan physician a few weeks before. She was a young, attractive woman, the beauty of her ebony skin heightened by the contrast with the stiffly starched white coat. Dr. Beverly, a name I remember, only because it is also the name of my only sister. I still don't recall whether it was her first or last name. She was either Jamaican-born, or a US immigrant of Jamaican parentage. But there was no smiley, tourism friendliness about this lady. She was seriously humourless, deliberate, and focused, ignoring my own nervous attempts to connect as a fellow-Caribbean … a stone-cold professional, that one. The kind of professionalism that I've since grown to love, require, and respect from my physicians.

"Whatever you're doing down there in Trinidad, you'd better get it together if you want to live," she chastised me, horrified by the reading of my elevated blood pressure. "There's a reason it's called the silent killer," she warned, unsmilingly. And so, on my return to Trinidad, where I was based at the time, in quiet desperation, I allowed myself to be talked into a reputable yoga class in a fancy suburb of Port of Spain, the capital city of the two-island Caribbean country that sits just seven miles northeast of Venezuela. I don't remember the brand of yoga, but the three or four classes I had attended seemed harmless, and if cornered, I could admit to beginning to feel some sense of calm and harmony that had been challenged by my re-integration into Trinidad society.

I had left the country of my birth in my late teen years "to further my studies," to use the then-language that applauded ambition and an appreciation of the importance of education and its link to upward social and economic mobility in a highly stratified society. Somehow, the expected four years had turned into an extended stay of post-graduate work, followed by interesting job assignments internationally and a New-York paced lifestyle. Yet, I had seemingly successfully managed the stress and maintained a normal blood pressure. Many thanks, I now realise, to my regular nightly tea of soursop leaves that are now popularized as an effective, natural soporific. Hence it became a mystery to the hyper-competent Dr. Beverly, as it was to me, that it was in returning to a supposedly less stressful lifestyle that there should be the threat of this silent killer that stalks the careless.

The yoga classes primarily involved breathing exercises and meditation practices that urged us to keep our minds blank. And then the kicker came. Arrival at a deeper level of cleansing, introspection, and self-connection required white clothing and the offering of a "gift of nature" to this guru. So, there was I in this long white dress, with my hand of green figs, freshly cut from my backyard, sitting in the yoga position on a colourful carpet in front of a life-sized photograph of a guru, also clothed in white. I can't remember whether I had completed the full time allotted for the blank-minded, deep-breathing exercise in front of the guru, or whether I had rudely interrupted the gems of peace and wisdom he was supposed to be communicating to me. I do remember that while driving home, without the green figs that were left as an offering, I self-checked: *"Girl, what on earth was that? You don't just have high blood pressure. You're going off your rocker!"* It was a literal "come to Jesus" moment when I self-admitted the need for greater spiritual grounding and guidance. It meant foregoing the exotic for the familiar ... going back to the basics.

Thus began my spiritual hunt for a deeper meaning to life. It was this search for purpose I was banking on to centre me in such a way that would steady my erratic blood pressure. And so began the quest that would lead through spiritual hills and valleys; roadblocks and guiding paths; questions, realisations, assurances; research, writings, discussions, and re-thinking religious experiences, present and past.

I had work to do and became an avid seeker.

*** *** ***

Guidance Text:
"But seek ye first the kingdom of God, and his righteousness; and all these things shall be added unto you" (Matt. 6:33).

CHAPTER 2
CHURCH INITIATION

As a child, my first introduction to organised religion was attending the Seventh-day Adventist church with my grandmother, Lavinia, popularly known as Miss Lilla. It was that introduction to the divine presence and guidance that would ground me, even when I strayed from physical church attendance. My mother, Sybil, had also been a practicing and active Seventh-day Adventist member but left the church at a point where she admittedly "looked around and saw nobody I wanted to marry." She then became an Anglican, aka Protestant. Perhaps there were no suitable interests there either, as she ended up marrying my father, Irving James, a Roman Catholic, promising to raise children in the Roman Catholic faith. Hence both my sister and I were sent to convent high schools after attending government primary schools.

Admission to a girls' Roman Catholic convent school at the age of eleven carried with it full participation of the rites and rituals of Roman Catholicism, with full focus on the catechism, the only route through which the Word of God was then communicated. There was no reading of the Bible, although for Scripture class there was the study of the Gospels: Matthew, Mark, Luke, and John, and the Acts of the Apostles. Soon there was First Communion, the invitation to participate in the Lord's Supper, and then confirmation, the infilling of the Holy Spirit. There were novenas and stations of the cross, the most interesting being the ones that involved off-campus bus excursions, and then the long climb up the Laventille Hill on the outskirts of Port of Spain to the Our Lady of Fatima shrine. In later years I would climb that hill many times to enjoy and support the Desperadoes Steel Orchestra, one of the premier steel bands of Trinidad and Tobago.

There had been a hurried and mumbled explanation of the non-use of the Bible, and an even more hurried explanation of the Crusades and other malfeasance of the Roman Catholic Church. Much later I would learn of the bold actions of Martin Luther and other Reformers who literally put their lives on the line to publicise and counter those malfeasances. As I write, Pope Francis has finally admitted that there is a "problem" with the sexual abuse of nuns, that even amounts to sexual slavery in some instances.[1] It saddens me yet emphasizes the key point, in my own readings and writings on gender and religion, of the urgent need for women to seek divine guidance from their Creator … not from human beings, who are innately fallible, nor from religious institutions which appear to be structurally and systematically misogynistic.

Church attendance on leaving school was routine, a sort of prophylactic covering designed to keep respectable girls out of trouble and give an appearance of holiness, without a truly transformative Divine connection. It was the time, though, of transformations in church liturgy, in the hopes of making the church more people friendly. To this end, an important change was the sign of peace, where the priest would give his blessing, then invite the members to communicate their pacific intentions through the shaking of hands. I remember thinking it a profound gesture, until I experienced it at a mostly Caucasian church in a predominantly Jewish and Italian neighbourhood in Brooklyn. At this point, I was attending school in New York, and lived in the Crown Heights section of Brooklyn around the time Whites were fleeing from the trickle of Blacks—mostly Caribbeans—who were threatening to flood the tree-lined streets with their colour and culture. It was the beginning of the white flight that characterized the housing issues of the time and would later turn Brooklyn into a throbbing, tempo-laden extension of the Caribbean. Interestingly, Brooklyn is now in the

---

1   Nicole Winfield, "Pope publicly acknowledges clergy sexual abuse of nuns," AP News, published February 5, 2019, https://1ref.us/wtw01.

centre of this cyclical dance of gentrification that is seeing the return of Whites.

But on the Sunday morning that I found myself at Mass in this Brooklyn neighbourhood in which I resided, it occurred to me that the sign of peace, which I had heretofore thought profoundly engaging, appropriately symbolized the hypocrisy that had begun to plague my understanding of this brand of Christianity. Before the Mass, I had encountered attendees who shifted their gaze from mine in order to avoid not only a simple greeting but the very acknowledgement of my humanity. This was the New York of the early seventies. Reluctantly, I stretched out my hand for the obligatory handshake, but that Sunday morning, I left Mass, silently vowing never to return to the Catholic Church. And I did not break this vow until many years later when I reluctantly accompanied a sister-friend in Nigeria ... a Yoruba Roman Catholic. Interestingly, she later came to her own come-to-Jesus moment and is the former pastor of a Full-Gospel Church in Lagos. The thought of returning to the Catholic Church went beyond my own horror and internal debate on the role of Christianity and the Roman Catholic Church in the enslavement of African peoples to a secular stance that seemed to be more in sync with my growing academic work. Still, it became more practical that any attempt at returning to organised religion would indeed begin with the Roman Catholic Church.

Bear with me as I reference my constant to and fro-ings, flashbacks, and "forwardings" between New York and Trinidad. At my home base in Trinidad, there was a lovely church, with an architectural design that I often admired in passing. I made a note to myself to do a drop-see one afternoon. That chance came sooner than I had planned, and on a lazy afternoon when I saw cars parked there, Spirit led, I dropped in on what turned out to be a midweek prayer session. The inside of the building featured an elegant display of white marble and anthurium lilies, further warmed by dimly lit candles. There were about fifty persons—mostly women—singing quietly, led by a youngish, beige-skinned woman strumming a guitar. My pleasant surprise was the upbeat tempo of the music. This was not the high church, Latin-language hymns with which I had been familiar. This was up-tempo, stylized Caribbean-influenced English hymns. I would later learn of a new movement within the Roman Catholic Church that sought to bring greater cultural relevance to worship experiences by indigenizing the music, rites, and rituals. There was also a deliberate emphasis on welcoming locals into the nunnery and priesthood. In my days at the convent high school, for example, all but two of the nuns were Irish. The few nuns and priests who were Caribbean-born, were second-generation Irish, often flaunting the privileged status that accompanied their white or near-white skin. This movement to indigenize church rituals was the result of the struggle against British colonialism that resulted in the independence of Trinidad and Tobago and many of the Caribbean islands in the sixties. Trinidad and Tobago, for example, achieved its independence in 1962, as did Jamaica.

All this to say there was and remains an interesting connection between Roman Catholicism and the quest for personhood in a post-colonial society that did not escape me that afternoon when I found myself back in a Roman Catholic Church, with the beige-skinned, youngish woman strumming a jumpy invitation to the Holy Spirit. I later learnt this was the beginning of the charismatic movement that would focus on an infilling of the Holy Spirit, talking in tongues, and a demonstration of divine power that allowed many to find more relevance and comfort in Roman Catholicism. Still, it forced others to seek a more authentic and spiritually powerful experience. Many found this in the evangelical churches, independent institutions that were widely dismissed as "small church" and considered beneath the status of those who found comfort, confidence, social mobility, and recognition through institutional power. I eventually would have my own "small church" experience, but that would be preceded by even more dramatic religious excursions as I sought a divine truth that I could wholeheartedly embrace. That visit sealed my final farewell to Roman Catholicism but accelerated a sincere push for an even deeper truth and recognition of the importance of purpose.

*** *** ***

Guidance text:
"[She] that dwelleth in the secret place of the most High shall abide under the shadow of the Almighty" (Ps. 91:1).

CHAPTER 3

FROM PLACE TO PURPOSE

Flashback to my New York sojourn, where my academic journey had continued to chisel away at the carefully engrained and orchestrated misconceptions about colonialism. It had been accelerated by a course on Caribbean literature—the irony of leaving the Caribbean to study about the Caribbean at a US educational instruction did not escape me. In fact, the anger I experienced further propelled me into Latin American and Caribbean studies, and then into a focus on anthropology. The quest for personhood and self-discovery had blossomed into an unapologetically firm and proud Afrocentricity. Its transference into religion, however, presented different challenges.

Despite a multitude of philosophical, political, and ideological excursions, I remained deliberately and steadfastly grounded in a Christian tradition. Needless to say, there were many questions that resulted in tremendous frustration, self-doubt, and serious backsliding, but my fundamental religious beliefs remained unshaken. Still, years later in Trinidad, when a friend invited me to attend a celebration of an Afro-centred religious group, I jumped at the opportunity. It was mostly curiosity and an opportunity to do my anthropology thing as "participant/observer." I searched my closet for my longest dress and matching headwrap—light on the makeup—to set off to meet my friend in the early night for the nearly three-hour drive to Trinidad's fascinating south.

After the long and mostly street-light deficient trip, we arrived at a spacious compound on almost three acres of land. There were several structures on the property. The first one nearest to the entrance was a large, well-lit, tent-like covered structure. I was struck that there were so few persons around on a night on which a major celebration was to have occurred; yet somewhat relieved that the event seemed to be not happening, since I had become overwhelmed with concern and apprehension during the long drive. But then we entered the first tent, to be greeted by the man who was introduced as the leader of the group. He was a sight to behold … a powerful, sturdy hunk of 6'3" ebony and wide … surely over 300 pounds, with huge, piercing eyes. I was almost paralyzed with fear. Surprisingly, he was quite welcoming, warm, and chatty to my friend, inquiring about our long drive and then beginning to explain the emptiness of the compound. He stopped suddenly in the middle of a sentence, looked at me, and somewhat derisively, commented that my eyes were as wide as saucers. My fear was by then no secret. It was clearly written all over my face. However, his teasing and explanation of the paucity of persons, helped to ease my anxiety. The women of the group had just returned from a pilgrimage and were still in isolation from the men and the rest of the congregation. Consequently, the night's celebration had been postponed. My relief was palpable. Much later my internal self-searching revealed that experience as a noteworthy example of the divine protection, even amid my innocence and ignorance. We were, however, invited to join the women in a smaller structure farther inside the compound, where there was passionate testifying about their experiences during the many miles covered on their pilgrimage. The women sang lustily and read Psalms. I was impressed that the Christian Bible was used and noted it as the syncretism that neatly folded Christianity into traditional African religion.

> *The night's celebration had been postponed. My relief was palpable.*

I had read some of Kenya's John Mbiti's work on African Religions and Philosophies (1969), in which he posits both Christianity and Islam as "traditional" and "African," in a historical sense, and lamented their representation as "foreign" or "European." I had begun to relate to God in the

African sense of the lack of separation between the sacred and the secular. God was interested in the mundane occurrences of my life as much as He was in my acknowledgement of His power and His guidance. This was the critical link of the purpose for which He had made and positioned me. "God is not pictured in an ethical-spiritual relationship with man. Man's acts of worship and turning to God are pragmatic and utilitarian rather than spiritual or mystical."[2]

Much later I would become acquainted with James Cone's theories of the "heresy of white Christianity," designed more with the purpose of controlling in order to conquer and subjugate than to direct to the path of true freedom: physical and spiritual. Cone, who declared his pride "to proclaim the gospel of black liberation from the margins of white culture,"[3] emphasises that "the central message of the Bible is God's liberation of the poor from oppression."[4] According to Cone:

> That theme is found in the exodus of ancient Israel from Egypt, in the prophets' message of justice, and most of all in Jesus's birth in a stable, his preaching of liberation and solidarity with the poor, and his death and resurrection. Liberation of the poor from the shackles of bondage is the central message of the Bible.[5]

To be truthful, that night there were no such intellectual ramblings on my mind. At that moment there were two important issues: 1) "How on earth did I get here?" And most urgently, 2) "How in the world do I get out of here—soon?!"

As many people do—particularly those of a certain age—I often look back on my life at the times God has intervened, often without my even asking. Surely that was one of those times. Immediately after the closing prayers and singing by the women, the leader of the women apologised that they were not able to entertain us, as they would ordinarily have done, because they were exhausted from their pilgrimage. They were very respectful of our two-hour drive back to the city, and quickly ushered us to our car. "Thank You, Jesus." My friend laughed at me all the way back to Port of Spain. I couldn't put my finger on it, but there had been an eerie vibe, and I remained stiff and traumatized.

---

2   John S. Mbiti, *African Religions and Philosophies* (Garden City, NY: Anchor Books, 1969), p. 6.
3   James Cone, *Said I Wasn't Gonna Tell Nobody* (Maryknoll, NY: Orbis Books, 2018), p. 80
4   Ibid., p. 81.
5   Ibid.

I don't recall the exact time—one month? Two months? Certainly, no more than three months later, the 6' 3," 300+ pounder of a leader with the piercing eyes suddenly dropped dead. Heart attack, the news media reported. Shortly after, no more than two months, his wife also dropped dead. I was stunned but did not try to internally process what seemed to be a mystery. My initial experience had permanently cured me of any forays outside of the Christianity into which I had been socialized. There would be, and there still are, questions, concerns, contradictions, disagreements, and internal arguments, but I was staying in my lane. The current mixture of hate, violence, white supremacy, and the deliberate distortions in the teachings of Jesus Christ by white, evangelical, extreme right-wing Christian nationalists were many years to come, or more accurately, to emerge from its feigned sleep. When it raised its ugly, divisive, hate-filled, and destructive head, I was filled with much of the guidance of the Holy Spirit and equipped to discern the spirit of confusion and the deliberate, direct, and demonic impact of the enemy.

Several months later, I visited a dear friend of my deceased mother in my hometown of Arouca, to invite her to a birthday luncheon for my sister. Teacher Merle, as we fondly called her, was in her garden lovingly tending her gerberas and roses. We chatted a bit, and she assured me she would be happy to come after church on Sunday because her church was not far from where I lived in the city. Now Teacher Merle grew up and lived about five minutes from the Roman Catholic Church, which I knew her to attend. She had taught and had retired as principal of the Roman Catholic school. Her father was what was respectfully referred to as a *porteglise,* one who frequented a church so often that he was usually the one tasked with opening the door of the church. The church was a five-minute drive from her home, a cool ten-minute walk, less if you took the shortcut through somebody's yard. Roman Catholicism was part of her legacy.

"You go to church in town now?" I asked, not even attempting to disguise my surprise. "Yes," she stood up and straightened her garden hat, "I go to the Trinidad Christian Centre. I am now a Christian." I was totally confused. Wasn't Roman Catholicism Christian? I wish I could remember her explanation. Whatever it was, it persuaded me to include the Trinidad Christian Centre in my quest. I did not know then, but that was a major step that would become the foundation of my spiritual journey, and lead to ongoing spiritual development. It remains a memorable green light in my journey **through** the wilderness.

Guidance Text:
"For I know the thoughts that I think toward you, saith the LORD, thoughts of peace, and not of evil, to give you an expected end. Then shall ye call upon me, and ye shall go and pray unto me, and I will hearken unto you. And ye shall seek me, and find me, when ye shall search for me with all your heart" (Jer. 29:11-13).

*** *** ***

CHAPTER 4
"SMALL CHURCH"

The church building was a tent and definitely not small. But the tent was the first thing that turned me off since in my limited experience, a "real" church could only be of solid bricks and mortar. It was a huge open but stable tent, well-located on about two to three acres of land. To my surprise, the congregation was from all appearances, middle to upper middle income. Women and men were well-dressed, even fashionably so. I recognised and greeted some of the local luminaries, many of whom were as surprised to see me there as I was surprised to see them. Much later I mused that heaven would be full of such surprises. I realised then that the term "small church," had nothing to do with the size of the church but churches that had made a clean break from the major established (read Colonial-influenced) Christian institutions: Roman Catholicism, Anglican, Methodist, Presbyterian, and other more recognized Christian institutions. The Seventh-day Adventist denomination would be placed on another mysterious level because of its Sabbath-keeping worship on Saturday, the biblically sound command of recognition of the seventh day of the week as holy and sanctified.

"Small church" appeared to represent a freedom from the status of the "recognised" Christian institutions and often did not share the same focus or concerns of those who were not near the top in a highly stratified society. It was the growth of these independent churches—fueled by an application of the gospel to an indigenous reality and pressing local issues—that brought about a new and more relatable representation of the gospel. Bear in mind that association with accepted Christian institutions was critical, often even essential to the status-conscious, preoccupied with upward social and economic mobility. All of this flashed through my mind as the tent began to spill over with Trinidadians of every stripe, representing the ethnic, social, political, and economic diversity of this multicultural Caribbean country, wonderful in its complexity, creativity, and challenges.

The musicians began to play, and a young Trinidadian woman of mixed ethnicity led out in the introductory praise and worship segment of the service. To my surprise, the beat was a more rhythmic and upbeat one that more closely reflected the Caribbean ethos than the often sleepy, Eurocentric church music to which I had been exposed. I was unfamiliar with the songs, but the words were simple, repetitive expressions of praise and exaltation of the Divine that I had never experienced before. A steel-pan soloist began to play a familiar hymn, possibly "Amazing Grace," and I knew I had entered the throne room. A young mahogany-toned pastor stepped up and gave thanks for divine provision and protection that had carried the congregation safely through the week. He prayed for the removal of any obstacle that would prevent the flow of the multiple blessings that a kind and loving God was about to bestow. There were loud hallelujahs and amen agreements from the congregation that had now reached standing room only. The divine service began, followed by more congregational singing. Then an olive-skinned, middle-aged pastor prayed and introduced the senior pastor, who then took the stage.

Pastor Bee[6] was a tall, dashing, beige-skinned man of mid-forties, his curly salt and pepper hair seeming to be out of place on his athletic frame. His impeccable dress made me uncomfortable ... too flashy, too much attention to detail, I judged. Someone pointed out his wife, a young, attractive near-white woman. For some unfathomable reason, I relaxed. There was a wife. *The presence of an in-house wife is comforting*, I rationalized. But then I learnt he was a local person who had recently returned from many years in Los Angeles, which perhaps explained the dapper dress. He was very smooth

---

6   *A fictitious name used to respect and protect the privacy of the individual.

… too smooth and as the Trinidadians would say, "my blood just didn't take him." In spiritual language, our spirits did not gel. The text used to ground the sermon still escapes me, as does the substance of the sermon itself.

But it must have been extremely compelling because I was impressed enough to return, and then to return again and again, struggling to subdue accompanying cynicism, and to ignore any evidence of the classism that stalked Trinidad's post-colonial history. Yet my spirit continued to reject Pastor Bee's dandy personality, even as he continued to impress me with his knowledge of the Word and to display a gifted, eloquent ability to simplify and communicate it. Stubbornly, or Spirit-led, I remained focused on my mission to discover/rediscover a spiritual centrality … to learn more about the God that I knew existed. I dismissed a gnawing discomfort with this eloquent pastor as the enemy of my soul that was determined to thwart my quest for a deeper truth.

My Sunday attendance at church service continued for several months. I was engaged, yet still questioning, determined to observe more carefully before fully committing. One Friday night I attended a prayer service. It may have been a week of revival, and the only Friday evening I attended. The tent was overflowing. I had arrived just in time to grab one of the few remaining seats on the outskirts of the tent. I don't remember the sermon, but after Pastor Bee's persistent call to action, I found myself at the front of the church with a crowd of folks responding to the altar call. The pastor began to pray over those who had come forward and then moved slowly to each person, placing his hand on their foreheads and praying fervently over them. What had I gotten myself into? There was no time for self-analysis, no chance of a quick exit. Before I knew it, with eyes closed, I could hear the pastor's voice next to me. Then his hand, cool and comforting, was on my forehead … and then I woke up on the floor of the tent, in my grey silk dress, with a covering over my legs that a church sister had carefully placed. I was "slain in the Spirit" as it was later explained to me.

> *I don't remember the sermon, but after Pastor Bee's persistent call to action, I found myself at the front of the church with a crowd of folks responding to the altar call.*

For several months, I continued to worship under the tent. Although based in Trinidad, I had been travelling quite a bit for work. Yet I would return to worship with this group every Sunday when I was in the country. My involvement with the congregation was limited, even as I was being schooled by the Word from the pulpit. One Sunday morning, as I entered, I was given a sheet of paper that turned out to be a survey that asked pointedly: "Do you consider Pastor Bee your pastor?" *What a question*, I thought. But the question became clearer during the service. Apparently there had been some ongoing, underlying friction—*bacchanal*, the Trinidadians would call it; *wahala* for the Nigerians—and those who considered the pastor to be their guiding force were urged to return the next evening to a special meeting to clarify issues. It sounded interesting, and I was curious. But thankfully I had an urgent meeting that conflicted with the scheduled time. Here is another example of the divine guidance at play, as would become clear so many times henceforth. Work travel interrupted, and I had no way of knowing what had transpired. But at the airport on my return trip, I ran into an ardent young man, who headed the children's ministries at the tent church. I stopped to chit-chat with him, only to find out that he no longer attended the church. What? He was one of the committed and highly prized young leaders. It was only then I heard that the meeting that I had divinely missed was so serious that it resulted in a major split in which two of the assistant pastors either left willingly or were fired. Each pastor was followed by members who supported them. Those who had agreed with Pastor Bee remained. My friend was on the opposing side and had instead switched his commitment to one of the other pastors. I got the address of the church he now attended, which was headed by one of the fired pastors. It was much farther from my home base than the tent church, but I found it. It was there, at the Agape Bible Ministries in Curepe, Trinidad, that I sorted out my major issues with organised religion and cut my baby teeth as a serious Christian, under the leadership of Pastor Samuel Philip. I would experience the wisdom of focusing on a "relationship" with God, not merely on "religion." Years later, my continuing issues with organised Christianity, and the increasing politicization and weaponizing of the word "Christian" would require me to clarify my identity as a "Christ-follower."

*** *** ***

Guidance Text:
"Therefore if any man be in Christ, he [she] is a new creature: old things are passed away; behold, all things are become new" *(2 Cor. 5:17).*

CHAPTER 5

THE JOURNEY NOW START

By profession, Pastor Samuel Philip was an educator, and he brought the clarity, patience, and courage honed in the teaching profession to his leadership of the Agape Bible Ministries. Pastor Sam, as he was fondly called, bore his six-foot presence with grace, humility, and none of the accoutrements of the pastor from the tent church or the swagger that had come to clothe men of the cloth with suspicion and mistrust. For weeks, and then months, I would sit quietly in the private school that had been rented for the Sunday morning church services with those who had followed him from the tent church.

First, we were about fifty, then 100, then 200+ and growing. The congregation grew and grew until we outgrew the school. The praise and worship at the beginning of each service brought a new understanding of the words "Spirit-filled." What I gained most, however, was a rock-hard, Bible-based Christian foundation, focused on God's love that surpassed all knowledge; my takeaway was a much-sought-after "peace of God, which passeth all understanding" (Phil. 4:7). The first time I attended an official Bible study, our "homework" was to read anywhere in the Bible and to return with a text that had particularly impressed us. My text was from Hebrews 11:6:

But without faith it is impossible to please him: for he that cometh to God must believe that he is, and that he is a rewarder of them that diligently seek him.

I was encouraged that Pastor Sam appeared to be impressed with the text I had chosen. Later came the understanding that the text remains one of the grounding Scriptures of the covenant relationship between God and humanity. In fact, Hebrews chapter 11 is widely known as the "faith chapter." Overall, I had no trouble with an intellectual grasp of the Word. Not much later, however, I would question the role of women in the church, *writ* large. It was a subservient role that that did not seem to be in sync with the loving God I was discovering between the pages of the Holy Book. It would lead to my writing two books on the subject, *Genderstanding Jesus: Women in His View* (2005) and *Genderstanding Leadership: Power to the Pew* (2013). As Spirit-filled as it was, however, the worship style at Agape Ministries presented a major challenge. I had been socialized into a crisp, formulaic, singing by rote, often replacing passion with joyless energy. At Agape, however, worship music was upbeat, and the words, simple, relatable, and meaningful, expressed praise, gratitude, love, and acknowledgement of a divine power that guides, protects, preserves, and blesses:

Thank you Lord
Thank you Lord
Thank you Lord
I just want to thank you Lord

You've been so good
You've been so good
You've been so good
I just want to thank you Lord

Lord I thank you for the sunshine
I thank you for the rain
I thank you for the peace in knowing, my trials don't come this day
And I thank you that someday soon, I got heaven to gain
I just want to thank you Lord

You saved my soul
You saved my soul

You saved my soul
I just want to thank you Lord

Thank you Lord
Thank you Lord (I just want to thank you Lord)
Thank you Lord
I just want to thank
I just want to thank
I just want to thank you Lord[7]

A huge screen at the front of the church scrolled the words to these songs. Not only did technology make a printed hymn book redundant, but it also left hands free to be raised and waved, while feet got "happy" in the kind of joyous praise that was totally unfamiliar to me. Years later, at a Mother's Day worship service at a Church of God in Riverdale, Maryland, I witnessed the Spirit leading the congregation into a "happy feet" worship for the entire service. Every time the pastor attempted to deliver the spoken Word, the church would be led into a session of corporate jubilation through dance. In 2004, to be exact, I would experience what may well be the wellspring of this joyous expression of praise and worship at the Action Chapel International Prayer Cathedral in Ghana, West Africa. Worshippers drummed, sang, and danced. An offering basket did not come to the congregation for their financial participation. Worshippers danced to the basket. Women, men, and children formed a procession and, in lively dance, moved toward the altar where they placed their sacrificial offerings. The dances became even more lively as members arrived at the location of the basket, where they twirled in reverent excitement before they deposited their gift.

Indeed, the alleged imposition of Christianity on Africa is one of the oldest myths taught ... that Christianity was brought to Africa by greedy enslavers and power-hungry colonizers. This strategic disinformation—okay, outright lie—and deliberate plan to mislead and deny African power and religiosity have impacted and impeded our worship experience.

In fact, monotheism—the worship of one God—existed in Africa before the arrival of European missionaries and enslavers and has been documented by many scholars.[8] Not only does Africa have a rich Christian past, but African Christians, also appalled by the mixture of truth and error

---

[7]   "I Just Want To Thank You Lord," Shazam, https://1ref.us/wtw02.
[8]   Burton, Cone, et al.

in the practice of western Christianity, now talk about the need for Africa to evangelize the West. What cannot be disputed is that an enthusiastic worship style, fueled by the rhythms of Africa have been traded for a staid, European worship style that has been force-fed, along with whitewashed notions of a Creator that sees Africans and people of African descent as stepchildren, if so much. Visual European representations of biblical characters that did not match the ethnic or geographic identities of those who inhabited that region of the world served to reinforce the lie.

All this to say, getting my stiff hands to raise in praise was a herculean task; to move my feet in tune to the lively praise songs being pounded from the piano or belted from the choir presented a measure of discomfort that forced another level of self-analysis. But I persisted and was rewarded with entry into a higher plane, a different level of spiritual intimacy with the divine power. I knew in my bones I had arrived. This is exactly what I had been missing. Exactly what I was seeking. And then I would truly understand the intersection of gender, ethnicity, and the impact of colonialism on my relationship to the divine power.

Several years of steady attendance and worship with the Agape Church followed. By then the church had grown by leaps and bounds. Soon we (I had become "we") bought and refurbished an old movie theatre, repurposing it into a place of worship large enough to accommodate the growing congregation. I was still trying to manage my lingering skepticism about organised religion and had ignored many calls for baptism. One day I finally answered that call. I chuckle now, because Pastor Sam himself expressed surprise, thinking that I had long been baptized. He had observed my attendance, as I had never missed a Sunday, as long as I was in the country. One Sunday, a friend whom I had invited to attend, unable to find me in the now-packed congregation, inquired of a member where I was sitting. She was quickly informed in the musical Trinidadianese: "She not here yet, but she coming. She coming late, but she coming." I did not disappoint.

It was June 1991. A warm Sunday afternoon, with the Trini sun bouncing its gleams off the blue waters of the swimming pool that would serve as

> *A warm Sunday afternoon, with the Trini sun bouncing its gleams off the blue waters of the swimming pool that would serve as the baptismal font.*

the baptismal font. Twenty of us were about to be baptized, with a matching number of supporters. There was singing and a brief word of introduction to our new walk when we emerged from the watery grave. Pastor Sam and a few of the elders got into the water and ushered the twenty of us into the water. The twenty baptismal candidates formed a semi-circle, as Pastor Sam offered a brief word that ended with a request that we confirm our intention. Then, one by one, he submerged us in the pool. I was wearing a long, white embroidered robe I had picked up in Senegal—not the same one I had worn to deliver my hand of green figs to the guru. Unsure about what the water would do to the cotton robe, and to guard against clinging, I had worn white, long tights underneath. When the water hit that cotton robe and tights, the weight of the confusion and chaos that had dogged me disintegrated, replaced by an indescribable peace and serenity. The sun overhead and the background singing witnessed the blur that encompassed me. I have no recollection of getting out of the water, changing into dry clothes, drying my dripping hair, or returning home for that matter. I was in a total daze.

Baptismal candidates from Agape Bible Ministries in Trinidad, W.I. The author is third from right.

Pastor Samuel Philip preparing the author for baptism.

Pastor Samuel Philip submerges the author in the watery grave.

Post-baptism celebration.

The following week had been a normal one, with no memorable distractions at work. That Friday afternoon, as I drove home from work, I felt nothing but peace … a soon-to-be-disturbed peace. As I reached my gate, my neighbour ran out to tell me she had been trying unsuccessfully to reach me at work. There had been a fire on a patch of dry grass beyond the fence at the back of my house. It was dry season in Trinidad, a time of the year that is usually flooded with bush fires. The fire had begun its devastating spread, so Ms. Neighbour called the fire department, who came promptly and extinguished the blaze. *Phew*! I thought and began to thank her. But she was not done. After the fire trucks left, she continued, she was looking through her window and saw smoke coming from my bedroom patio. Under her amazed gaze, the smoke increased. In a heightened state of panic, she again called the fire department. They returned quickly, identified the fire on the patio, and completely extinguished the fire, without breaking into the house. At this point, I ended the conversation abruptly and ran into the house to see the damage. All seemed fine, until I opened the door and stepped onto the patio. The fire had seemingly started from a spark from the first fire and caught a cotton hammock, which was now partly burnt. But that was not all. The flames had reached the ceiling, coming perilously close to an electrical connection.

It was not until at church that Sunday, when Pastor Sam introduced the baptismal candidates to the congregation and inquired whether anything extraordinary had happened, that I made the connection. Pastor Sam's eyes widened as I related my story. Only then did I understand the reality of spiritual warfare. I was on the battle ground. My baptism had angered and awakened evil forces. I had picked a side. The spiritual warfare was on, but it was a fixed fight. My Bible had well-documented and recorded a divine victory. The battle was already won. But the journey had just begun.

*** *** ***

Guidance Text:
"For we wrestle not against flesh and blood, but against principalities, against powers, against the rulers of the darkness of this world, against spiritual wickedness in high places" (Eph. 6:12).

CHAPTER 6
THE NEARNESS OF GOD

My heart was set. I was all in. However, there was one major concern that kept tugging at me. Would I still be permitted to dance? Go ahead and laugh if you wish, but for me this was a serious matter. To be truthful, I, too, had not realised how serious it was. I am a Trinbagonian first and foremost. "Trini to de bone," they call people like me. And for us, dancing is a genetic predisposition. According to family lore, I danced as soon as I could walk, much to the shock and amusement of my parents, who could not determine the source of my dance influence as they were by no means party people. My own memory is that of a ten-year-old being urged to teach my brilliant cousin, several times my age, to dance, as he prepared for his wedding day. A handsome, over-achieving attorney and pharmacist, poor Cousin Lloyd stepped over his own two left feet, tying up my little feet. He did not do much better the day of his wedding either.

The Trinidad and Tobago Carnival is the platform for the collaborative, public display of the dance, embedded in the Trinbagonian genetics for generations. When I grew up, in those days of waning colonialism, "decent people" did not participate. I had a different view that focused on the protest, rebellion, and struggle for identity and personhood embedded in the Carnival and was bold enough to warn my parents that once I was away at school, I would return every year to participate. They ignored my teenage musings, but once I graduated and became somewhat self-sufficient, I kept my promise, aided by the free ticket from my father's airline employment, for which I still qualified. I saw the historical, revolutionary, culturally affirming, and freeing function of the annual two-day pre-Lenten festival as a symbol of liberation and national pride, more than the spiritual contradictions. Long story short, with some difficulty I gave up "playing mas" or actively participating in the two-day festival. But the thought of not being able to dance again remained a haunting bugbear. I discussed it with no one, fearing it might have been considered frivolous, even coming close to being sacrilegious. In fact, I did not even think it was an important enough issue that warranted prayer. But the God I came to know, and was indeed becoming even closer to, not only knows our inner thoughts and desires, but He also seeks to supply every need. Indeed, He says: "Before they call, I will answer; and while they are yet speaking, I will hear" (Isa. 65:24). The God I came to know intimately answers prayer even before we ask. In His love and omniscience, He anticipates our every need, and in His omnipotence, He is able to deliver. Hallelujah!

And so not too long into my internal struggle with the appropriateness of dancing as a Christian, I attended the wedding of a childhood family friend. Teacher Merle; remember her? She was the family friend from whom I had first learnt the difference between Roman Catholicism and Bible-based Christianity, a discussion worthy of its own book. Indeed, she had been one of my carefully chosen spiritual guides. A mentor for many of us, she was in full attendance at the wedding. The reception included great Trini food, and of course, pulsating, tempo-laden Trini music. As I sat and gingerly tapped my feet, Teacher Merle got up to dance. What! I watched in amazement as she did her lovely two-step move to the calypso. It was a move I would later see her do quite sedately Sunday mornings during the praise and worship at the Agape Church, where she also worshipped. Before I knew it, I was on the floor doing my own thing in a relief that truly came from the soul. It was as though the doors of my soul had been flung open; a yoke severed from my neck; a burden cast off my shoulder, allowing full and authentic self-expression and joyful representation of my identity. The same experience would later be transferred to the worship experience.

My experience in traditional Roman Catholicism—before the more enlightened and spirited charismatic movement—was one of silent, quiet, repetitive prayer. As I mentioned earlier, when I first attended the Agape Bible Ministries, my hand sat stiffly at my side. Not for anything could I "command my hand to praise the Lord," as one of the praise songs went. My feet were wooden, equally defying the commands that my brain could not send. It took more than a year before I could distinguish between secular dancing and the dance of praise.

This pitiful self-containment is deeply lodged in a history of exploitation, subjugation, and control experienced not only by the biblical Israelites but also by past and continuing attempts to erase the identity of God-loving people of colour. The re-definition and re-direction of worship was a strategic intent of the colonial agenda that coupled with and utilized Christianity to subjugate and make more malleable its captives. It is laced with a Eurocentric perception that only European-styled worship is acceptable. **Breaking News: God is not European**. Moreover, many people of colour and non-European Christians have accepted and internalized a notion of the "devilish" nature of any worship music that does not come directly from a European hymnal. Mercy! This thinking has restricted our perception of God; silenced our worship style in music; restricted our ability to worship in dance, and stifled the creativity of experiencing and spreading the good news through music: "Bless the LORD, O my soul: and all that is within me, bless his holy name," says David in Psalm 103:1. How much are we missing as Christians to dismiss, devalue, and even deplore dance in worship?[9]

As I grew in Christ-centred maturity, I would read of the importance of praise dance in both the Old Testament and the New Testament. According to the text in ***Exodus 15:19–21***, as the waters of the sea parted to allow the dramatic crossing of the Israelites on dry land, Pharaoh's horses, chariots, and riders were not that blessed. Called to resume their position by God, the waters obeyed to cover and drown the pursuing enemy. Aaron's sister, Miriam, a prophetess, took a tambourine and led the women singing and dancing in a celebration of victory.

Sing to GOD—
What a victory!
He pitched horse and rider
Into the sea! (***Exod. 15:21, MSG***)

---

9 Editor's note: While praise dance has scriptural precedent, it must be recognized that a counterfeit style of praise is prevalent in the last days. Spiritual perception is needed to discriminate between godly and ungodly worship dance. See these writings from E.G. White: 2SM 36:2; ST May 20, 1880, par. 2; and 23LtMs, Ms 115, 1908, par. 77–81.

It is worth noting that the women were the ones who were documented as dancing. Are we to understand that there was a gender component to praise dancing? That would easily be dismissed with another dramatic documentation of praise dancing, this time by a male, King David. Not only did David dance, according to the Word, he danced before the Lord with all his might **(2 Sam. 6:14-22)**.

Overwhelmed with joy because of the return of the Ark of the Covenant to Jerusalem, David jumped and leaped and twirled. He somersaulted and his outer garments revealed his gold satin knickers. He whirled again and this time, he danced out of his outer regal garment, the heavily embroidered purple and gold overcoat that established his royal identity. David was deep in joyous praise. He was not concerned about his status, his image, how he would appear, or what others would think and say. He was deep in a praise zone.

The uninhibited victory celebration of God's presence and guidance is only half of this amazing story. The other half is the response David received from his wife, who had observed his performance from her balcony. It is one of the most instructive examples of the difference between the assessment of humans and God's view of us. To say that Michal, David's wife, was not pleased would be a gross understatement. She was downright embarrassed … "despised him in her heart" (2 Sam. 6:16) is the biblical explanation.

According to the text **in 2 Samuel 6:16**, Michal detested David's actions, believing his dancing to have been beneath his royal status. "How glorious was the king of Israel to day," her words dripped with sarcasm, "[uncovering] himself to day in the eyes of the handmaids of his servants, as one of the vain fellows shamelessly uncovereth himself" (2 Sam. 6:20). David, however, was brusquely clear in his unrepentance. Fully grounded in his faith, he declared that he would display his total allegiance and commitment to God through his dance, showing his thanksgiving for the kingship the Lord had bestowed on him. But he was not finished. He declared his intention to continue to rejoice and praise through his dancing, even if he looked foolish. I often muse at the many saints afraid to dance because well-coifed hair would be disarranged, or—horrors!—fancy hats shift from their lofty perches.

The text, in **verse 23**, ends with a stark warning to those withholding their praise:

"*Therefore Michal the daughter of Saul had no child unto the day of her death.*"

It remains unclear as to whether Michal became barren as punishment, or whether David, in total displeasure, avoided the matrimonial bed and the execution of his matrimonial duties.

I often wonder whether failure to praise with the dance is punished by bodily pains or arthritis. The advice of the psalmist, however, remains clear: *(Ps. 149:3–5).*

Let them praise his name in the dance:
Let them sing praises unto him with the timbrel and harp.
For the LORD taketh pleasure in his people:
He will beautify the meek with salvation.
Let the saints be joyful in glory:
Let them sing aloud upon their beds.

Truth be told, I am unable to delink the blatant rejection of the praise dance by the powers that be in most churches from the history of Christianity and enslavement. So much has been documented about the imposition of Christianity on the enslaved Africans for the specific purpose of enforcing their subjugation. For example, the drum and other musical instruments were banned, as singing and dancing were deemed suspicious. With good reason, since these were often the basis of escape plots and a means of communication. With good reason also, since religious strategies used to restrict and contain the enslaved were often turned on their head and formed the basis of ploys to obtain their freedom. In the preface of his important work, *The Black Church*, Henry Louis Gates, Jr. writes:

> "The miracle of African American survival can be traced directly to the miraculous ways that our ancestors—across a range of denominations and through the widest variety of worship—reinvented the religion that their "masters" thought would keep them subservient."[10]

Drumming and dancing were perceived as some of the most subversive elements, as were many forms of celebrations and gatherings. No wonder I am still often shy and reluctant to dance in church, especially if aided by music that supports my reluctance. But when moved by the spirit, I cast off the lingering bonds and dance, although, sadly, not yet as spirited as King

---

10 Henry Louis Gates, Jr., *The Black Church: This is Our Story, This is Our Song* (New York, NY: Penguin Press, 2021), p. xxiii).

David. Still, I have already signed up for the dancing section in heaven, and several friends have planned to meet at the Judah Gate.

God be praised!

*** *** ***

Guidance Text:
"Let the high praises of God be in their mouth, and a two-edged sword in their hand" (Ps. 149:6).

CHAPTER 7

GROUND ZERO: FAITH AND FAVOUR VERSUS FEAR

In the thirty-fourth Psalm, David encourages us with the reminder that the eyes of God are always upon the righteous (verse 15). As a baby Christian, I still had a lot of work to be "righteous," but my new commitment or re-commitment took me to the Genesis text: "Fear not: for am I in the place of God?" (Gen. 50:19). It directed my memory to those moments when I knew for sure that His hand had always been on my life. It is a worthwhile exercise for all Christ-followers, at whichever level of the journey, to reflect on the many ways in which God had guided, protected, and provided for you.

About a decade before my return to Trinidad, I was returning to New York from the Cote d'Ivoire (Ivory Coast) on the west coast of Africa, where I had been on a rather hectic assignment. This was the era in which the DC10 planes had been experiencing several problems, and I had driven my secretary crazy with instructions not to book me on a DC10 flight. Alice succeeded with the outgoing flight, but she had no control of the return trip.

At the gate for the late-night flight, the plane loomed large and imposing in its DC10 glory against the black velvet night. It had been a long day; I was too tired to fuss, and goodness knows when I would have been able to secure a seat on another flight. I boarded, found my seat, took off my shoes, asked the flight attendant for some *chaussettes*, buckled my seat belt, and went to sleep. Takeoff found me deep in la-la land. My cold, naked feet woke me up, without a clue as to how long I had been asleep. I rang the bell to summon the flight attendant, at which my seatmate, who appeared to be an African diplomat, looked at me with eyes as large as two white saucers. Another man in the seat ahead and across the aisle looked back with equal shock. He was Caucasian, but he seemed unusually pale. I later identified it as unveiled fright.

> *In the thirty-fourth Psalm, David encourages us with the reminder that the eyes of God are always upon the righteous.*

The flight attendant appeared and informed me, quietly, but crisply: "*l'avion est en panne.*" "*En panne?*" I repeated sleepily. "*Oui Madame, nous sommes retournant a l'aeroporte.*" It took me a while to unravel the French, and then slowly the horror of the English translation flooded my mind: *Broken....* The plane broke? I also understood that we were returning to the airport. My seatmate with the saucer-white eyes looked at me silently. He uttered not a word. Interestingly, my first reaction was to search for my shoes. If I had to go down, I would need my shoes. I couldn't swim, so apparently I was planning to walk on the water. The next move was to pull up the window shades, gingerly, to peep through the window, without appearing to panic. Everyone in the cabin appeared to be putting on a brave front, and I didn't want to let down the side. But since I was on a plane that was *en panne*, and returning to the airport, I needed to see lights through that crack in the window. Even more gingerly I peeped: black velvet. I lifted the window shades a bit higher, but the darkness was blinding. I closed my eyes tight, clenched the arms of the chair, and a biblical text often quoted by Iris Randall (RIP), a spiritually centred colleague, quieted me: "Be still, and know that I am God" (Ps. 46:10). Those were the words that filled my soul with peace and comfort for the next ten to fifteen minutes … the lifetime it took until the captain's voice interrupted the studied silence to announce our landing.

There had been no applause after we landed. Everyone filed out in stoney, silent order, still shocked by the ordeal. The cacophony erupted as we entered the safety of the departure lounge. African women fell to their knees in loud praise and thanks, while their men attempted to retain a brave front. European men cluttered in a corner recounting the events, their wives, with blanched faces, seated on the nearest chairs. From the bits of information I gathered from the many versions I could hear, there had been a loud explosion, and the plane took a long dive downwards before levelling off and turning for its return trip to the airport. My saucer-eyed seatmate quietly informed me that he had held on to my hand, trying to wake me, but, in full sleep mode, I didn't budge. I parked my shudder of being held by a male seatmate while I slept soundly for self-analysis and deep thought at a more opportune moment. I was too busy giving thanks for not having the experience of a plane in free-fall … especially at a high travel phase of my professional life.

The title of a sermon I once heard is: "Remember Not to Forget." It emphasized the importance of reflecting. Sometimes it takes many years to fully comprehend what God did, but it is always an intense comfort to remember that He is always in charge. And how often we forget. Constant and deep reflection is one of the major foolproof strategies for checking one's spiritual journey. It has a way of humbling you beyond your own recognition of yourself, and, even more critically, directing you to the real power in your life. My own reflections continue to lead me to the divine forces of protection and preservation. Later, my journey to Christian maturity would focus on spiritual strategies for protection and preservation. One such strategy was to clothe myself in the protective armour of God.

That strategy would serve me well. No more than seven years after returning to Trinidad, my then husband died suddenly from an asthma attack while on a work assignment in Belize. That episode is another story that revealed the long arm of God's everlasting grace and presence in my life. As the shock of his passing waned, a sense of aloneness and vulnerability increased. I was now living alone and fearful with three dogs: two noisy and entitled Caribbean terriers (Ju-Ju and Mau-Mau) and Matador, a German shepherd that flaunted the size and beauty of a lion. The house was alarmed to the teeth. Under my bed, I was packing: a hammer, a cutlass (aka machete), and—laugh if you must—a wooden rolling pin. A can of mace and a whistle were at hand. I was ready for war.

This overwhelming sense of vulnerability called for a firm plan of action. After one of Pastor Sam's inspiring sermons, I memorized **Ephesians 6:11-17:**
The King James Version reads:

> *Put on the whole armour of God, that ye may be able to stand against the wiles of the devil. For we wrestle not against flesh and blood, but against principalities, against powers, against the rulers of the darkness of this world, against spiritual wickedness in high places. Wherefore take unto you the whole armour of God, that ye may be able to withstand in the evil day, and having done all, to stand. Stand therefore, having your loins girt about with truth, and having on the breastplate of righteousness; And your feet shod with the preparation of the gospel of peace; Above all, taking the shield of faith, wherewith ye shall be able to quench all the fiery darts of the wicked. And take the helmet of salvation, and the sword of the Spirit, which is the word of God.*

A strategic plan to move from a consultancy to more structured working outside of the home had thrust me into the daily day-to-day confrontation of the challenges of life in the hustle and bustle of Caribbean drama. Previously, my consultancy had afforded me an opportunity to be selective about time and place for local travel. Now, I was in the middle of the mix. When I left for work on mornings, as I got into my car, I would suit up spiritually: "On my feet, the preparation of the gospel of peace; the loin cloth of truth; the breastplate of righteousness; the shield of faith to protect me from the fiery darts of hell; the helmet of salvation, and the sword of the Spirit, which is the Word of God." It became my road march. I learnt, too, an important lesson: when the Holy Spirit says, "Move," you move. Don't argue. Don't hesitate.

One steamy day in July, it was the Friday of a long, tiring week. I had worked through lunch and conducted some difficult meetings. I started to open a file to do some more work, and the Spirit said to me, "You should go home now." I was a bit hesitant to leave, but I was tired, and I had a weekend of more work planned. I was a practicing Christian, but not yet a Sabbath-keeper. I got the necessary clearance from the CEO, then headed out of the office, about 3 p.m.

Now in Trinidad and Tobago, the official work hours are from 8 a.m. to 4 p.m. My office building was in the heart of the downtown area, busy, but within easy reach of everything. I headed to the bank. The bank was crowded. It was the end of the month when most people got paid. *Not today*, I thought. There was a persistent urge to get out of town. *I will find another bank on my way home.* I walked quickly to my car, parked in the garage of the Old Library Building that had been occupied by the Trinidad Theatre Workshop. As a then-member of the board, I had been allowed to park there. The Old Library Building is situated opposite to the Red House, the country's then-seat of administration ... comparable to the Capitol Building in Washington, D.C. I got my car, waved merrily to the garage-keeper, and drove out of town to a bank closer to home. I had never been to that bank before but had often passed it. There were a few people in the bank, so I went in, conducted my business, and got out of there in record time. As I hurried out, I noticed a supermarket next to the bank. I had never shopped there before, but I could see that the supermarket was also empty, surprising for a Friday afternoon at the month's end. I popped in to pick up one item. Spirit-led, the one item led to badly needed, full-blown shopping. But it was still early before the Friday 4 p.m. traffic madness. I headed west, homebound, and there was another surprise: only one car in the usually crowded gas station. I was almost home, and with only a quarter tank of gas, I went in to fill up. Farther down the road, the flower vendor was unloading his beauties at the side of the road, so I stopped and treated myself to my tropical faves: anthurium and ginger lilies. Back on the road and near the turnoff for home, I decided to skip the bakery, and the pickup from the cleaners and headed home. I am ahead of the game. Home free. My intention was to get a quick nap, then write through the night to meet the deadline on a consulting project.

Sleep came easy and sweet, before being interrupted by the ringing of the telephone. But the sleep was sweet. Before the machine could pick up the call, the phone stopped its shrill noisiness, then began to ring again. I did not answer. It rang again. Quickly after, the gate bell rang. "*Steuups*. I can't even sleep in peace," I muttered as I peeped through the window, and saw my next-door neighbour in an unusually harried state. I rushed to the gate to hear the news: **"There is a coup in the country."**

From the hill on which she and I stood, we could see black smoke billowing from the capital, Port of Spain, in the centre of town near the office building I had just left and the bank that I had thought too crowded to remain to conduct my business. We could hear explosions. We heard gunshots. We ran back inside and locked our houses, where we were forced to stay until days later, when calm was restored. There had been no television reception. The television station was under siege. Seventy-two rebels had stormed the Trinidad and Tobago Television and held workers hostage. The radio would later deliver a sketchy report that a homegrown, radical Islamist group had staged a bloody coup. The location was the Red House, the Seat of Parliament. The attempted coup had been launched from the Old Library Building, across the street from the Red House, where my car had been parked. On the other side of the street, the police headquarters had been burnt to the ground. *Ground Zero.* Newspaper photos later showed the cars of my colleagues, parked at the Old Library Building, completely riddled with bullet holes. My car had escaped it, only because I had promptly obeyed that internal voice.

The news media later reported that more than 100 members of the group had stormed the parliament building. The then prime minister, A.N.R. Robinson, had been beaten, shot, and held hostage with most of the members of his cabinet in the Red House for six days as violence and looting erupted in Port of Spain and the surrounding areas. The downtown area I had just left was in the middle of the mele.

The country had remained completely on lockdown for six days. Nothing moving, except the looters who braved the moment. Supermarkets were closed and remained closed for many days. No food. Thanks to my unplanned shopping spree, guess who had food enough to spare. My girlfriend and I laugh that she still owes me a chicken. Some twenty-four persons had been killed, including a member of parliament, and many more had been injured, with millions of dollars in property damage.

When all of that pandemonium had been taking place, guess where I was—in my bed, taking an afternoon nap, with cash, enough food to "lend" a friend a chicken, a full tank of gas, and flowers to calm my spirit. **What an awesome God we serve!** He watches over us and protects us even before we know we need protection.... That is the *"secret place of the most High, under the shadow of the Almighty,"* of which the psalmist speaks in Psalm 91:1. The Message Bible says: **"*That's right—he rescues you from hidden traps, shields you from deadly hazards. His huge outstretched arms protect [us]—under them [you/we are] perfectly safe; his arms fend off all harm."*** Amen?

When I left my home that morning, having donned my Ephesians 6 armour.... When the Spirit told me to leave the office early, guided me away from the crowded bank to my car that had been parked on **Ground Zero**, directed me to a bank I had never used before, but adjoining a supermarket that enabled me to stock up on food; to have a full tank of gas; to get flowers, to even get in a good nap, because there was little sleep for the next week, I had no idea I was being guided away from **Ground Zero**.

That is what the theologians call: prevenient grace … the grace that goes before us. The unmerited **favour** that surrounds believers. It is as though we are moving in a bubble of grace. So why should we fear? The Message Bible continues in Psalm 91: ***"Fear nothing—not wild wolves in the night, not flying arrows in the day, not disease that prowls through the darkness, not disaster that erupts at high noon."***

And verse 3 of Psalm 27, my grandmother's favourite Psalm, provides the bold assurance that ***"Though an host should encamp against me, my heart shall not fear: though war should rise against me, in this will I be confident."*** Hallelujah! One of my favourite texts is ***2 Timothy 1:7***: **"For God hath not given us the spirit of fear; but of power, and of love, and of a sound mind."** We often focus on the power and the love but overlook that "sound mind." It takes a sound mind to listen, to obey, and to move. When the Spirit tells us to move, it is to move, without question or understanding. We are living in perilous times when we will be required to make quick decisions that would determine our spiritual, mental, and physical security. There will be little time to dither, to rationalize, or to negotiate with God. In fact, we may not even be able to use our Bibles, so we have to hide the Word in our hearts.

Our prayer life must be intentional and not optional. We have to be:

1. **Prayed Up** … pray without ceasing.
2. **Trust and Obey**: *"Trust in the Lord with all thine heart; and lean not unto thine own understanding. In all thy ways acknowledge him, and he shall direct thy paths.*
   (Prov. 3:5-6).
3. **Listen and Act**: Trust requires obedience and action.
4. **Move!!!** Move without looking back. Remember Lot's wife? She turned into a pillar of salt.

But this is not only for our safety and security. Others are looking at us, and looking to us, as Christ-followers, for their guidance. It is a tremendous responsibility, but a tremendous opportunity to witness. At the most perilous point of the COVID pandemic, a girlfriend of mine WhatsApped me with this note: "I have never felt the panic and anxiety of this pandemic. But I have an inner peace, and I am making use of this time creatively. There is too much life to live to spend it being afraid." But here is her last sentence that really stirred my soul: "All these Christians who love Jesus, but are afraid to meet him." These are the words from a non-Christian woman.

These are confusing times for the best of us. One does not have to be a believer to grasp the drama that is unfolding in our world. Most folks know something big is happening that they cannot explain. They are looking at Christ-followers to critique the way we are responding but also to be guided by our actions. When we leave church, WE ARE the church.

Let us not be afraid of the uptick in random violence, racism, white supremacy, police brutality, or anti-democratic ploys that are opening the doors to totalitarianism. God's love drives out and displaces fear. Let us suit up with the whole armour of God so that we could stand against the wiles of the devil and **move** out in His strength with holy boldness, not hiding or panicking, but seeing our lives as points of contact for others to access God. Fear and faith do not make good roommates. Fear cuts us off from our source of strength and hope. It isolates us; immobilizes us; paralyzes us; wears us down. Our faith is the antidote to fear. So let us not give the enemy room to control our thoughts and our mind. Y/Our mind is the battlefield where the war against fear must be fought. We must be sensible, aware, equipped with the Holy Spirit's understanding and discernment of every situation and constantly praying. We have to build ourselves up with the Word of God, led by the Holy Spirit, and bringing **every** negative thought into captivity. God has given us His spiritual armour for our protection, but we must put it on. Every piece has been designed to guard and protect our minds.

The Girdle of Truth; the Shield of Faith; the Breastplate of Righteousness; the Helmet of Salvation; the Gospel of Peace; and the Word of God, which is the Sword of the Spirit.

Peter, writing to believers who were distressed at the trials they were going through, warns in **1 Peter 1:13**:

"Wherefore gird up the loins of your mind, be sober, and hope to the end for the grace that is to be brought unto you at the revelation of Jesus Christ."

The Message Bible makes it plain:

"So roll up your sleeves, get your head in the game, be totally ready to receive the gift that's coming when Jesus arrives."

We're in the middle of war. Spiritual warfare. And our victory lies with the powerful spiritual weapons God has given us. So let us suit up, with His whole armour, and shelter under His amazing, saving grace.
HALLELUJAH!

*** *** ***

Guidance Text:
"Because thou hast made the Lord, which is my refuge, even the most High, thy habitation; there shall no evil befall thee, neither shall any plague come nigh thy dwelling. For he shall give his angels charge over thee, to keep thee in all thy ways" (Ps. 91:9–11).

CHAPTER 8
THE INSIDE ENEMY

As we make our decision to follow Christ, the evil one goes into full-throttle attack. One of the plans of the enemy is to keep us so busy looking for the enemy on the outside, that we neglect the necessary internal monitoring and self-evaluation, consequently overlooking the enemy inside.

My revelation of this particular strategy of the enemy came during a casual Trini Sunday lunch: stewed chicken; stewed fish; macaroni pie, Calypso rice, green figs, sweet potatoes, dasheen (aka provision), and callaloo—a spicy green blend of the leaves of the dasheen, ochroes, and a bit of pumpkin and coconut—swizzled to a remake of *Ewedu*, one of the culinary delicacies retained from the Yoruba of Nigeria and appropriately revered as the national dish of Trinidad and Tobago. Over the dessert of coconut/pineapple ice cream, topped with a pomerac sauce, the conversation veered to puzzling, other-worldly experiences. After carefully listening to other stories, I timidly offered two experiences of being in that liminal phase between sleep and wake and feeling a force pushing down on me. On both occasions, in terror, I repeatedly mouthed His name: "Jesus. Jesus." The force released me. The experience had remained as inexplicable as it was unspeakable. I did not know what it was, but I knew it was not good. I had successfully erased it from my consciousness until that Sunday luncheon.

My cousin, an elderly relative at whose home I was lunching, calmly inquired as to whether my house had been blessed. I had never thought about it before, but to my knowledge, it had not. "You need to get that house blessed," she said. A proactive woman of God, she immediately arranged for a lay pastor from her church to do what she strongly felt was needed.

The pastor of the Full Gospel Church where she served as an elder was a young, dynamic man whom I had not previously met, but I trusted her and agreed. Not only did she set up the house blessing, but she also attended, arriving in a separate car from the pastor. We sat in the living room and chatted a bit about my new spiritual life and prayed. The young pastor then walked around the house, inquired about a few African sculptures, then asked to see where I slept. I led them upstairs to the bedrooms. However, at the top of the staircase, there was a small alcove that held a writing desk and two bookcases. The desk was strategically placed under a window that provided a full view of the approach to the house. The pastor paused: "What goes on here," he asked? "This is where I work most of the time," I replied casually, beginning to explain that not only did I have a full view of anyone approaching the house, but I could also be inspired by the view of both the valley and the sea. He was not impressed. In fact, there was concern on his face. "Do you have olive oil?" he interrupted. "Yes," I said. "Bring it," he commanded. I descended the stairs on wobbly knees, rummaged through kitchen cabinets for the olive oil and returned, my shaking knees barely carrying me up the staircase. To this day, I do not remember or did not see what the pastor did with the olive oil, my eyes were so tightly closed. As I matured as a Christian, I would learn that the oil represents the Holy Spirit that brings knowledge, truth, grace, and the love of God. I do know that the pastor prayed long and fervently, then asked to be directed to my bedroom.

One of the plans of the enemy is to keep us so busy looking for the enemy on the outside, that we neglect the necessary internal monitoring and self-evaluation, consequently overlooking the enemy inside.

His had become a piercing silence. When we reached my bedroom door, before we even entered the room, my cousin's eyes locked on a piece of sculpture I had bought on one of my travels. She inquired about the history of the piece. I could barely remember but searched my mind for its provenance. I thought it was an unusual piece. I had purchased it from an art market in one of my travels and had placed it over the bedroom door for several years. I noted that there were other pieces downstairs which didn't seem to have warranted her concern. "Get rid of it," she said. "In fact, give it to me. I will get rid of it." No problem. I got the piece down from its perch and surrendered it to her. The pastor remained quiet, silently praying throughout this exchange. I was still somewhat frozen from the olive oil drama.

"You have a friend," the young pastor suddenly came alive. "A woman who is very close to you." I waited patiently for more information, since I had many female friends who were very close to me. With eyes half-closed, he proceeded to describe this woman. I gave him a blank stare. He was not to be distracted or deterred. He continued with a full description: height, complexion, hair style. I screwed up my face, bit my lip, scratched my head, and thought as hard as I could, running through the list of close friends, near and far, old and recent. Not a soul came to mind. No one fit the description.

"Never mind," he relieved my anxiety. "Don't worry. It'll come to you. However, when it does, know that she is not your friend." Now I was really worried.

He proceeded to examine my bedroom, and thankfully, found nothing objectionable. He prayed again for my protection and left with my cousin. But the most uncanny aspect of this whole experience was still to come. As soon as the gate closed behind both cars, it was as though a veil had been lifted from my eyes. The identity of the "friend" who was declared to be a non-friend came to mind. It was indeed uncanny that this "friend" was the one person the computer of my mind did not upload as I sorted through the names of close female friends. The accuracy of his description and my inability to make the connection were astounding. I sat on the bed, shuddering, mulling over the reason the loyalty of this childhood friend should be suspected. I could find no reason, but I took action. After closely monitoring subsequent events, I managed to strategically distance the friendship.

Coincidence or not, I never again experienced another nighttime liminal visitation. At least not a negative one. One night, however, I suddenly awoke to a presence in the room. I could sense the exact location of the presence. But instead of the feeling of dread and terror that I had experienced before, I was flooded with an overwhelming sense of peace and love. It was as though a shower of warm, fragrant water was being poured over me. I have long searched for the words to describe that experience. I have never found those words, because to have related that story to anyone would have positioned me as unhinged. But if pressed for a description, I could only think of colours … soft, fragrant, rose-pink hues. To date, it is my closest encounter with heaven on earth.

Another of those inexplicable incidents occurred with a young woman I had invited to attend church. She had been a co-worker who had joined a small lunchtime prayer circle in my office. The CEO had soon shut us down, apologetically explaining that because mine was a management position, I could be accused of either intimidating staff who did not attend or currying favour with those who did. Still, the young employee accepted my invitation to attend church. I would pick her up every Sunday morning, take her to church, then return her to her home where she lived with her parents. Interestingly, she never sat with me at church. She would wend her way to the back of the church, while I sought a seat somewhere in the middle, out of the range of the over-competent air conditioner. Every Sunday, as Pastor Sam did the altar call, I would force myself to keep my head forward, determined not to look back at my friend. Often, I would shut my eyes and command them to remain closed, as I prayed that she would be one of those walking up the aisle to the altar to accept Jesus Christ as her personal Saviour. Sunday after Sunday, she ignored the altar call. On the way home, I mustered every ounce of discipline to resist introducing any conversation about her reluctance to respond to the altar call. This continued for several months, possibly a year.

One Sunday morning, I do not recall—or choose not to remember—what drama was going on in my life, but I just could not muster the energy to go to church. This was quite unusual, since I enjoyed the praise and worship session, the sermons, and fellowship with members of the congregation, some of whom had become good friends. Not so this Sunday. The spirit was willing, but the flesh definitely did not get the memo. I was not merely lethargic; I was physically weak and did not think I could gather enough strength to even get out of the bed. After much internal argument, I determined that if I could force myself out of the bed to get a cup of tea, I could summon the energy to get dressed. The challenge, however, was getting down the stairs to the kitchen to make said tea. I struggled for several more minutes. Finally, I stumbled out of the bed and literally crawled down the stairs to the kitchen, where I mustered all my strength to make myself a cup of tea. It was energizing—well … slightly. A timely phone call from Dee reminded me that she was expecting me to pick her up to go to church. And so, I did, however late it was.

That Sunday morning, we did the usual. I found a seat in the middle of the church; Dee secured one at the rear of the church. I don't recall a word of the sermon, except that it was a spirited one. Still, the enemy was on the warpath and had managed to put me fast asleep. I stirred after the altar call. When I opened my eyes, there was Dee, standing at the altar, accepting Jesus Christ as her Lord and Saviour. I could not believe my eyes. Much later in the day, as my usual energy returned, I detected that the force that tried to keep me from going to church was defeated by God's overcoming and prevenient grace—the divine favour that goes before us—that saved my friend that Sunday.

The enemy suffered a tremendous loss that day. Not long after, Dee brought her father to church, and he eventually became an elder. Soon after, her mother followed, waving a banner every Sunday to present her burden for Trinidad and Tobago, the country she loved so much that had been battling its own challenges. Both of Dee's parents have passed on—as well as the beloved Pastor Sam—but she has remained faithful and passionate on her spiritual journey, often encouraging me. Glory hallelujah!

What an awesome God we serve!

*** *** ***

Guidance Text:
"And thou, Solomon my son, know thou the God of thy father, and serve him with a perfect heart and with a willing mind: for the Lord searcheth all hearts, and understandeth all the imaginations of the thoughts: if thou seek him, he will be found of thee; but if thou forsake him, he will cast thee off for ever" (1 Chron. 28:9).

CHAPTER 9

POWER IN THE BLOOD

Stories are important testimonies. They enable us to review our lives and to reflect on the many ways and times in which we have been protected in this cosmic struggle between good and evil. "Reflection faith," Dr. Wesley Knight of the Revision Church in Atlanta calls it. We have that extra covering of protection once we have a relationship with the Divine.

The aforementioned experiences, and many others, too numerous to mention, ushered in a sense of safety and that of operating under a protective covering that dwarfs the perpetual fear of any sensible woman operating in a man's world … a "hedge of protection" as the Bible would describe it (Job 1:10). How else could I go to sleep (okay, with one eye open) with a huge tarantula in one corner of the ceiling of the room I slept in while on a research trip in Africa? Or not bat an eye (okay, I was shivering with fear) as I was gingerly transferred to another vehicle in the middle of an African jungle as my own research vehicle got a flat tire? Or having arrived one day early for a meeting in then-Communist China, take a taxi in the growing dark to the meeting site two hours away as we communicated through the only word he knew in English: "Okay?" And my one-word Mandarin response: "Okay!" It is only as a maturing Christian that I now identify the peace that passes all understanding and binds all fear when under the coverage of the powerful blood of Christ.

Years ago, my friend, Faye, who lived in New York was visiting a friend of hers in Washington, DC. Faye had agreed to accompany her to a wedding in Virginia, since the bride had kindly extended the invitation to her. It was an elegant, outdoor southern wedding on a bright summer day, and a good time was had by all. On their way home, as they were discussing how lovely this wedding was, Faye commented: "That was such a beautiful wedding … but did you notice that we were the only Blacks there?" Her friend looked at her in amazement. "Are you kidding?" she replied. "Everybody there was Black, except for three or four persons. That was a totally African American wedding."

In the United States the "one drop rule" also known as the Hypodescent Rule—dates to a 1662 Virginia Law that defined a Black person as anyone with a drop of Negro blood. (The word *Negro* was used at that time.) The rule meant that any degree of African ancestry would classify the person as Black, with the unequal status it carried at the time, a presumed inferiority that still lingers in the minds of many. Apparently, all the guests at that wedding had only a little more than one drop of Black blood. (I grimace at the idiocy of the concept of "Black blood," with the full knowledge that there is one race, the human race.) But to get to the point of the story, all the guests physically appeared to be Caucasian but identified as Black, either by choice or by force.

To be truthful, I have always found this one drop rule to be particularly ridiculous and somewhat hilarious. While the concept of the one drop rule was designed to prove the inferiority of the blood of Africans and peoples of African descent, it seems to suggest quite the opposite, if one wanted to go down that road. The theory is supposed to be a powerful weapon against Blacks. Yet, if one drop of blood could decide one's ethnicity, and overrule the other 99%, that is mighty powerful blood. It led me to thinking of the blood of Jesus and the amazing power and strength of the blood that was shed to save us. Hallelujah!

A well-known hymn asks the question:

"Would you be free from the burden of sin?
Would you o'er evil a victory win?"[11]

---

11 "Power in the Blood," Hymnary, https://1ref.us/wtw03.

and then states emphatically:

> "There is pow'r, pow'r, wonder-working pow'r
> In the blood of the Lamb;
> There is pow'r, pow'r, wonder-working pow'r
> In the precious blood of the Lamb."[12]

This hymn should bring us all great comfort in these perilous times. We are now on this grand cosmic stage in the deadly crosshairs of the battle between good and evil, between love and hate. Some of the experiences described before point to the indisputable fact that I was, and continue to be, in the middle of a war ... the war between good and evil. It is a war in which we are all involved, whether we acknowledge it or not. The age-old war between Jesus Christ and Satan.

The war, both physical and spiritual, is brought to us in living colour in the choices made in television programming. I would see it in the deterioration of human relations in Trinidad and Tobago; in glaring oral depravity in electoral debates both in Trinidad and the US; in the re-definition of truth and the normalization of lies ... lies creeping into policy decisions that affect the lives of the global community, especially communities of colour. It would be clearly visible in the confusion, chaos, and unimaginable incivility, with scarcely disguised support and encouragement to white supremacists. It would be transparent in the selection and election of people to major leadership positions in the US and around the world ... a grand display of the biblical warning of "spiritual wickedness in high places" (Eph. 6:12). And then at the time of this writing, I would see it every day, as we battled the deadly but invisible COVID-19, and bear the passing of loved ones, even as we suffered through the mixed messages on vaccines. Many still experience the chaos in financial insecurity as they are confronted with the loss of employment, housing, and health care.

It is clearly visible in the politicization, monetization, and the weaponization of religion in the deliberate misrepresentation of biblical principles. In some religious circles, the words "social justice" have become fighting words, with one pastor unbelievably criticizing Jesus for being "weak." Help us, Lord!

We see the banning of books in attempts to erase history and the call for the halting of much-needed racial sensitivity, diversity training, and

---

12   Ibid.

affirmative action in government, business, and education. We continue to experience systemic racism and its related violence and police brutality. We feel the hostility in the air from those who look down on the blood of diverse humanity as if it is different from theirs.

We are dodging hurricanes, storms, floods, fires in California, even paradisical Maui, earthquakes in Haiti and Morocco, devastating flooding in Libya, heatwaves in Europe, even as global warming and climate change are denied. But even as we tangle with these wiles of the devil, we must be strengthened and comforted in the knowledge that we not only carry more than one drop of His blood in our spiritual DNA, but as true believers, we are totally covered by the blood of Jesus. And yet, even one drop of His blood would be sufficient to cover us. Blood that was shed specifically for your salvation and mine. HALLELUJAH! The Bible is laden with promises contained in the New Covenant of our redemption and salvation that have been sealed with the blood of Jesus.

> *The Bible is laden with promises contained in the New Covenant of our redemption and salvation that have been sealed with the blood of Jesus.*

In Exodus 12:13 (ESV):

"The blood shall be a sign for you, on the houses where you are. And when I see the blood, I will pass over you, and no plague will befall you to destroy you, when I strike the land of Egypt."

In Hebrews 10:19–20 (ESV):

"Therefore, brothers, since we have confidence to enter the holy places by the blood of Jesus, by the new and living way that he opened for us through the curtain, that is, through his flesh."

In Ephesians 2:13 (ESV):

"But now in Christ Jesus you who once were far off have been brought near by the blood of Christ."

In his message to the Ephesians, Paul emphasizes the transforming work of God in our lives, which we should not take lightly. We should also not take lightly our responsibility to share it with others.

The Message Bible (Eph. 2:11–13, emphasis mine):

But don't take any of this for granted. It was only yesterday that you outsiders to God's ways had no idea of any of this, didn't know the first thing about the way God works, hadn't the faintest idea of Christ. You knew nothing of that rich history of God's covenants and promises in Israel, hadn't a clue about what God was doing in the world at large. Now because of Christ—DYING THAT DEATH, SHEDDING THAT BLOOD—you who were once out of it altogether are in on everything.

The question remains: How do new Christ-followers participate in the creation of one new humanity? The responsibility is undeniable, and so we must move out in confidence, calling on the blood of Jesus not only to cover us in these desperate times but to be a guide to others. However, first we have to be sure to cover ourselves with the blood of Jesus not only to protect us, strengthen us, and give us the courage to operate in a dangerous world. Remember that once we declare ourselves as Christ-followers, others are watching us. Often the way we deal with difficulties is a more effective witness than we could even think. Those of us who follow Christ are walking sermons. Even without our knowledge, some folks are going to be taking their cues from us. It is an awesome responsibility, especially in the midst of these dangerous times, but we all have work to do.

Paul reminds us that in addition to having work done in and for us, we have to be active participants in this urgent work at this crucial time. As we cover ourselves with the blood of Jesus, let us be bold to share the good news to others that they, too, can share in this great glory of God's goodness, mercy, guidance, and saving grace.

One of the main strategies of the enemy is to steal our JOY…. But we are blood-bought, freed, and entitled to express our joy in the Lord. To sing a new song. To worship. Do not let the enemy steal your joy … and do not let the enemy prohibit your praise dance.

Here is an effective action plan:

- Acknowledge that we are in the middle of an ongoing war.
- Cover ourselves with the blood of Jesus as we navigate these tumultuous times.
- Fight with confidence because we are in a fixed fight that we have already won. The battle was won on the cross.
- Share the good news of His saving grace with others.

There is such a reluctance to listen to Christ-followers now—thanks to the hypocrisy of the Christian right—that we must design new plans and strategies for witnessing to others. Let us remember the price that was paid for our salvation, and the power in the blood that covers us. It is surely more than one drop, but even one drop of the blood of Jesus would be more than enough.

Thank You, Father! Thank You, Jesus.

*** *** ***

Guidance Text:
"But now in Christ Jesus you who once were far off have been brought near by the blood of Christ" (Eph. 2:13, NKJV).

*** *** ***

CHAPTER 10

OUT-OF-PLACE WOMEN

Women activists in Jamaica sing a song that encapsulates women's increased activism and leadership, particularly in this period of world's history.

Women time a come, oh yeah (make e come,
make e come, make e come,) Oh yeah![13]

It is sung in the Women's Movement throughout the Caribbean, encouraging women to step out of the traditional second-hand role and place imposed on them and to step into their purpose. Study of the Word introduced me to the many representations of women in the Bible that, to my mind, questioned the seeming strategic plan of most organised religions to silence or downplay women's roles by erasing them from sermons, discussions, writings, etc. These actions appeared to challenge or undermine the purpose of women or to limit them to subservient roles. My spiritual journey took me to a deeper knowledge and understanding of the special place in the heart of God for women, and the specific role He has carved

---

13 This song probably originated in Jamaica, W.I., and has served as an anthem at Women and Development meetings attended by the author. A search for publication information yielded no information.

out for us. It is a role that is in constant conflict with a world structure that continues to subordinate women. This realization led to a pervasive question: *"What Does God Want from Me?"* It is a question that has haunted me and one we should all be asking ourselves—whether female or male; old or young—especially since we are undoubtedly living in the countdown to the second coming of Jesus Christ.

What then was the purpose for which I was created? What "fruit" should I be bringing forth? Despite the horrible worldwide news and the blatant attack on women's rights, it is also a time when women's voices are finally beginning to be heard. Once upon a time, it was customary and acceptable for women to be told to get back in their place when they appeared to be moving out of spaces to which they had been traditionally confined. Now, however, women's voices are being heard, and women are stepping out of their place and into greater leadership positions. My encouragement for all women—young, old, and in-between—is to **step out of your place and into God's purpose!**

> *What then was the purpose for which I was created? What "fruit" should I be bringing forth?*

When I think of women stepping out of their place and into their purpose, I think of the numerous courageous women to be found in the Bible. Women who stepped completely out of their place, sometimes in desperation to get help for themselves. Some examples are the woman with the issue of blood, courageous and persistent in her search for healing; or to show gratitude for forgiveness as Mary Magdalene; or to demand that her Son take shame from the face of the peasant household when their wine ran out as Mary, the Mother of Jesus, did at the wedding in Cana; or to accept the important mission of spreading the news of the gospel as the woman at the well; or to save their cities as the wise woman in 2 Samuel (20:16–22). Then there are Abigail and Esther, moving with holy boldness to save their people. My book, *Genderstanding Jesus: Women in His View*, documents the various instances in which Jesus directly addressed women's subjugation and suffering. In addition, it reveals Jesus' tendency to break through social, cultural, and religious traditions to exonerate, liberate, and empower women.

We often overlook the importance of the Old Testament, but it documents God's intention and support of women's equality in order to enable their full participation. The fact is, the Old Testament is revealed, explained, and confirmed in the New Testament. One story is very clear about God's concern about women. In patriarchal Israel, only males were permitted to inherit property. If a man had no sons, his land was passed through the other males in the family, usually his brother or uncle. Too bad for his daughters. Anthropologists call it patrilineal inheritance, a practice that still exists in many cultures today. These are long-established forms of ordering and managing societies. People have little choice of whether to comply or not. But in Numbers 27, the daughters of Zelophehad, who had no male siblings, and were faced with the death of their father, decided to take matters into their own hands. Sister Mahlah, Sister Noah, Sister Hoglah, Sister Milcah, and Sister Tirzah thought it was unfair. They did not grumble or gossip. They openly but respectfully challenged the system.

The daughters of Zelophehad were bold to even think of challenging tradition. They were bold even to think of entering this space before Moses and Eleazar, the high priest, and all of the congregation. Holy boldness. They stood at the door, because it must have been a sacred space, in which women were forbidden to enter. I believe those young women had a direct relationship with their God, a holy, fair and just God, that they knew they could approach. Hallelujah! They knew their God would listen, even when they could not approach men, and their God came through for them.

> **"The daughters of Zelophehad speak right: thou shalt surely give them a possession of an inheritance among their father's brethren; and thou shalt cause the inheritance of their father to pass unto them"** *(Num. 27:7).*

Not only did the Lord agree, but He also made it law.

> **"And it shall be unto the children of Israel a statute of judgment, as the LORD commanded Moses"** *(verse 11).*

Hallelujah!

And this is not just biblical history or Anansi story. Several years ago, while working on a gender and development project in a West African country, the driver of the organisation for which I was working shared with my colleague and me that a few years before, he had overheard women delegates who were attending a similar meeting talking about ownership of property by women. He had three daughters, and since there were no sons, he became suddenly aware that at his death, his land would have gone not to his daughters but to his brother, who would then pass it down to his own sons. Patrilineal inheritance. After overhearing the discussion of the women, he made haste to divide his property, ensuring that each daughter got her share in her name. This one small act would ensure his daughters' ownership of property, the ticket to financial and social stability. A pretty revolutionary act.

I have to confess that I hooped and hollered when I first read this story, and I still want to kiss the Bible every time I read this story in Numbers 27:1–11. It is not an aberration when we turn to the New Testament and see Jesus going out of His way and taking special care to include women; to teach them; to engage them in serious discussion; to counsel them; to heal them; to empathise with them; to empower them. He promoted women's dignity and equality in very demonstrative ways. Perhaps He expected them to have a more active and significant role, as they did in the early church. In fact, in His concern for the spiritual, physical, and intellectual lives of women, Jesus made a clean break with Judaism by taking the time to teach women the meaning of the Scriptures. It is by design. It is intentional, because Jesus was woke! It is a term that speaks to an awareness of gender inequity, racism, classism, and the struggle for social justice, diversity, and inclusion.

Indeed, in spite of many gains made—some of which are now being deliberately and strategically revoked—women continue to be marginalized and frustrated in efforts to help to transform society through substantive participation in the building of God's kingdom. Yet the Word in **Acts 2:17–18** says:

> **And it shall come to pass in the last days, saith God, I will pour out of my Spirit upon all flesh: and your sons and your daughters shall prophesy, and your young men shall see visions, and your old men shall dream dreams. And on my servants and on my handmaidens I will pour out in those days of my Spirit; and they shall prophesy.**

In a few archaic religions, women are still being directed to "stay in their place." In those religions, that place is to be any place but the pulpit. And while I indeed believe in the doctrine of the priesthood of **all** believers, and that certainly includes women, those of us in the pew still have real work to do. In fact, there is an increasing need for women to take on new challenges and to become change agents.

*So, "What does God **really** want from **me**?"* First of all, the fact that an all-powerful God wants and expects something from little, inconsequential me is as intimidating as it is humbling. In his popular book, *The Purpose-Driven Life*, Rick Warren asks the question: "What on earth am I here for?" And then he continues, shockingly: "It's not about you." He completes that first paragraph with the central theme of the book: "If you want to know why you were placed on this planet, you must begin with God. You were born **by** His Purpose and for **His** purpose."[14]

It is critical that every girl and woman remember this fact, especially when society appears to be deliberately rolling back the rights of women. Despite all the gains made, there is an outright attack on women and persistent efforts to keep women out of place and out of the fulfillment of their divinely ordained purpose, whatever that might be. Many call it **kingdom-purpose**. It is an appropriate term. Because it is in focusing on this kingdom-purpose that we find the divine power to lead out in situations that would surprise even our own limited minds and dim opinions of our abilities. For many women, the connection of faith and feminism can be elusive, and perhaps for many more, even counterintuitive. Largely it is a failure to interpret feminism as a deep understanding of the structural subordination of women, that is to say, the ways in which society has been organised around keeping women in a secondary and unequal role and place. In fact, "Christian feminist activists, linking the personal and the political to the spiritual, have begun to question the failure of development programmes to connect and include women's spirituality, and to stress the importance of spiritual development to the success of development programmes."[15] On the other hand, woven into the fabric of many religious organisations are systems and practices bent on maintaining male-dominated power and control and undermining women's contributions to the church and to society.

I keep thinking that the fact that we are all here at this particular time in world history, when all the signs are pointing to the final drama, means that God thought us all—women and men—so special that He has hand-picked, prepared, equipped us, and hardwired us for such a time as this; for a specific purpose that only we can fulfill. No one can replace you to fulfill the specific purpose for which you have been created. You and I are all standing in the gap: between right and wrong; between good and evil;

---

14   Rick Warren, *The Purpose Driven Life* (Grand Rapids, MI: Zondervan, 2002), p. 17.
15   Meryl James-Sebro, *Genderstanding Jesus: Women in His View* (New York, NY: TEACH Services, 2003), p. 2.

between decency and indecency; between civility and vulgarity. Each one of us, female and male, has been specially selected to do something that only we can do; to reach someone that only we can reach. To accomplish something only we can accomplish for the kingdom.

We are the ones. We, women and men, who are Christ-followers, are called to represent. So how do we do that? It calls for a reality check that focuses on what we bring to the table. The key word is PURPOSE. What is our purpose? We are chosen, as the text says.

> *"I have chosen you, and ordained you, that ye should go and bring forth fruit, and that your fruit should remain: that whatsoever ye shall ask of the Father in my name, he may give it you"* **(John 15:16).**

Now does that mean that unanswered prayers can be linked to un-purposed lives? It is something to ponder, but it certainly calls for a reassessment of our God-given talents and a re-thinking of direction. Yet to put a bow on it, there are no un-answered prayers. God either says: "Yes," "No," Wait," or "Change Direction, Just Trust Me."

We are again reminded in 1 Peter 2:9, that we are a chosen people. The Message Bible provides a true understanding of this text:

> *"But you are the ones chosen by God, chosen for the high calling of priestly work, chosen to be a holy people, God's instruments to do his work and speak out for him, to tell others of the night-and-day difference he made for you—from nothing to something, from rejected to accepted."*

So many of us quit even before we start, because we can't do this, and we can't do that. We don't have the experience; we don't have the knowledge; or we're too busy; or we're shy. Consider the servant with the one talent, from Matthew 25:14–30 and Luke 19:11–27, who saved it carefully, did nothing with it. Why? He said: "I was afraid, and went and hid thy talent in the earth" (Matt. 25:25).

Fear is a paralyzing trick from the pit of hell. I know the talent in this text means money or treasure, but if we were to take it literally, how many of us are hiding our talents and abilities because of fear? But the Word clearly states that He has not given us a spirit of fear, but of power, love and a sound mind (2 Tim. 1:7). In addition, if you are unsure or in need of guidance, ask for wisdom. God will grant it to you generously (**James 1:5**). That's our God! Large and in charge.

The key challenge in finding that purpose is to do a self-assessment of the things we like to do; the things we think we are good at; the things we seem to have a natural ability to do ... even if by doing it, we might be considered "out of our place." These may well be our spiritual gifts we need to identify, acknowledge, and nurture with the specific purpose of using them in the work for which we have been appointed in these last days.

Some pastors have developed the acronym SHAPE to help to determine our spiritual gifts. They urge us to be persistent in examining our SHAPE:

S – Spiritual abilities ... from God for you to share and serve
H – Hearts ... special passions God has given to you
A – Abilities ... talents God gave you from birth
P – Personality ... the special way God has wired you
E – Experiences ... our past that God uses for today

These spiritual gifts are neither for us nor about us. They are for the purpose of accomplishing the work of the Holy Spirit. My own journey continued with the challenge of encouraging myself to **get in SHAPE**, and more critically, to **stay in SHAPE**. Spiritual shape. Again, my constant concern remains: *"What does God want from me?"* The answer can only come from submission to His will and staying focused and vigilant in the face of distraction, discouragement, and fear, even rejection. Remember *"For God has not given us a spirit of fear, but of power and of love and of a sound mind" (2 Tim. 1:7, NKJV).*

Let us give thanks to the Lord for placing, protecting, providing, preparing, and equipping you with special talents for such a time as this.

Perhaps of greatest importance and urgency was the need and the desire to search the Scriptures for myself, not depend on someone's interpretation of the sacred texts and to depend on the Holy Spirit for guidance to a deeper understanding and its specific application in my life. I started with the King James Version, then got every version I could find that gave me a better understanding ... even a New Testament translation in Gullah, a gift from my sister. Know that when you ask the Holy Spirit to open avenues through which you might develop and express your God-given talents, to find and fulfill your purpose in His Service, it is a serious prayer! Be ready to submit yourself to

Dr. Dorothy Height, 1912–2020 (centre) renowned social justice activist and president of the National Council of Negro Women for forty years, introducing the author (extreme right) to African dignitaries in New York.

divine direction … and be ready to be taken places and serve in areas that you didn't even imagine, areas for which you may think you are not qualified. The first time I agreed to preach, my throat was so dry that I thought I would faint … right in front of the congregation. God does not call the qualified. He qualifies the called. Remember, God could have chosen anyone, but He chose *you*. But for what purpose?

I recall the day after Kamala Harris was announced to contest the election as Joe Biden's pick for vice president, her sister, Maya Harris posted a picture of both sisters as young girls, captioned with a quote from their mother: "Don't let anyone tell you who you are. **You** tell them who you are."[16] I would add. "You show them **whose** you are by carrying out His purpose in your life." Amen?

Let us give thanks to the Lord for placing, protecting, providing, preparing, and equipping you with special talents for such a time as this. Ask

---

16 Maya Harris (@mayaharris_), "'Don't you let anyone tell you who you are. You tell them who you are.' - Dr. Shyamala Gopalan," X, August 12, 2020, https://1ref.us/wtw04.

for divine help in finding your purpose, guidance, and the Holy-Spirit power and courage to fulfill it in the mighty name of Jesus.

RISE and SHINE!

*** *** ***

Guidance Text:
"Ye have not chosen me, but I have chosen you, and ordained you, that ye should go and bring forth fruit, and that your fruit should remain: that whatsoever ye shall ask of the Father in my name, he may give it you" (John 15:16).

CHAPTER 11
RECHARGE YOUR BATTERY

The Christian journey is by no way a direct path, free from obstacles. In fact, it could very well be described as an obstacle course. Sanctification is life's journey: day by day, one step at a time. There are highs and lows, ups and downs, moments of feeling one has arrived at the highest point of spiritual connection. Very often, as one begins to enjoy a comfortable spiritual cruise, there is a sudden plunge into limbo lows, with the need to jump those spiritual canals. My limbo lows have been many. The most memorable, however, was the sudden passing of my then husband of seven years from an asthma attack. But even in this most traumatic period of my life, the hand of God was present.

I was at home alone when I received the call of his untimely passing while on a work assignment in another country. As I reached for the phone to call my only sister, who lived in New York, I realised I would be unable to reach her because at that very moment she was on a flight to Trinidad for vacation. It was then I knew that God would guide me through this difficult period. And, indeed, He did. He had already put things in place so that I would not be alone. Prevenient grace.

Managing the first year of widowhood is a story that truly deserves its own book. It was a time of loneliness, depression, and extreme uncertainty, yet rich in self-discovery and a closer recognition of divine guidance. Work and church took over my life, and I thank God for those close "friends" who distanced themselves—and the loyal friends and new acquaintances who provided support and encouragement.

After a year of widowhood, a gentleman I met through work became an overly interested suitor. He was a mature Christian, intellectually stimulating, and lived in another country. But perhaps because of his own hectic travel schedule, he was too eager. It was an eagerness that I found unsettling and viewed as a potential spiritual trap. The situation soon required more than the average prayer. I approached my heavenly Father with the holy boldness He requires of us and asked for a sign. Surely, He knew how visual I was and how unobservant I could often be. *"Lord, I need a clear, dramatic sign for your direction,"* I pleaded.

I returned to New York that year to spend Christmas with my sister and my nephew and to consider returning to a New-York-based life, which was still a viable alternative. My eager suitor was on his way to a business meeting somewhere in the Pacific and decided to break his trip for a quick New York lunch. I selected the venue, a safe mid-Manhattan restaurant on Madison Avenue, where retired ladies with pearl necklaces met their girls before or after a day of museum hopping or shopping for things you could tell they clearly did not need. More importantly, the location allowed me enough time to scoot over to a dental appointment across the street. Lunch went well as he spoke about the many meetings that had been arranged. The efficient waiter brought the bill, and he reached for his "bro bag" or *sacoche* as the French call it.

Empty space. Yes, I had seen it slung across his shoulder, European style, as he entered the restaurant. Yes, he had placed it on the back of his chair. No, neither of us had left the table. Now, however, the bag had vanished into thin air. We raised an alarm at the restaurant. Sure enough, there had been a rather busy busboy, who had also vanished. The mystery lad had cleared the table with a huge black garbage bag in his hand, which I had noted as unusual for this swanky mid-Manhattan restaurant. As the restaurant manager attempted to sort out the situation as surreptitiously as possible so as not to disturb diners, but also to protect the reputation of the restaurant, my luncheon date tried to come up with a plan to quickly replace his identification, credit cards, and especially his passport and travel documents so he could travel to his meeting. Then he dropped the bombshell. There was also a diamond and sapphire necklace and earring set in the bag. It was to be presented as an engagement gift for his intended proposal. I froze. Not because of his intention or the magnitude of the loss. It was the dramatic answer to my prayer. Had I not been convinced before, I now knew for sure that GOD WAS AND IS REAL AND THAT HE IS A GOD OF HIGH DRAMA.

God hears and answers prayers. In fact, I couldn't help but marvel at God's sense of humour in wanting to make sure that my eyes were not dazzled by the sapphires, my favorite stone, so the jewelry disappeared even before I could set eyes on it and be tempted to make the wrong decision. I once heard a prominent pastor declare that when you pray and see your prayer answered for the first time, it scares you for life … in a good way. The Message Bible refers to it as "reverential fear" (Luke 1:65, MSG). It is the confrontation of the truth of God's reality that is the "no-turning-back moment." For me, it is the truth of God's presence in my life that continues to help me jump those pesky spiritual canals.

For many folks, limbo lows may not be as dramatic as the sudden passing of a loved one, or they may be even more intense. These spiritual challenges could be as seemingly simple as the argument with a best friend, the loss of a job, searching for or adjusting to a new home, a family dispute, disappointment of some kind, or something as mundane as overwork or a bad hair day. It is then that you see the powerful and unmistakable hand of God in your life. It is then that you know that—similar to any cell phone or computer—you need to recharge. Recognizing the need to recharge is half the battle. How to recharge is a strategy everyone must devise for herself and himself, even before it occurs. It is called being battle-ready. It begins and ends with knowing His promises of assurance that are ubiquitous in His Word.

The takeaway, however, is that personal crisis, as difficult as it was, strengthened my spiritual connection and grew into a greater involvement with a supportive church family. The hand of God guided me through that low and, five years later, into the arms of a man on a similar spiritual journey. Even the confirmation that he was divinely sent has its own stories. The most dramatic, however, is my accompanying him to a family gathering for a graduation celebration in Michigan. We were not yet married, so I shared a bedroom with his mother, who had also been visiting.

One morning, Mama Sebro solicited my assistance in calling a friend and asked me to get her address book. It was a medium-sized, bright red leather address book: *Hmmm pretty spiffy for an elderly woman*, I chuckled to myself. But as I flipped through the pages for her friend's number, I saw a handwriting that looked somewhat familiar. I soon realised it resembled my own impossible scribble. I flipped again and saw the name and number of a person I knew, and then confirmed that it was indeed my handwriting. "Mama," I said trying to control my astonishment, "where did you get this address book?" She furrowed her brows as she ran it through her computer-sharp mind. "Oh, I was collecting things for our Dorcas Society sale, and Leola gave it to me. I liked it so much, I bought it." Now, the said Leola is a dear friend, and I had indeed given her some items to add to her collection for the rummage sale. But all of this had occurred a long time before I had even met this man to whom I was at that time betrothed. At the time of this writing, he remains my husband of thirty plus years. Glory to God!

The most efficient way of becoming battle-ready is through the Word. Gather and memorize texts of encouragement to prepare you for the heat and protect and support you through the fires. One of my "road marches," as I call them, is the guidance to suit up in battle gear as outlined in Ephesians 6 and as I detailed in chapter 7. In the mental and spiritual preparation for marriage, I also leaned heavily on Proverbs 3:5–6. It continues to support me through the ongoing challenges of married life: **"Trust in the Lord with all your heart, and lean not on your own understanding; in all your ways acknowledge Him, and He shall direct your paths"** (NKJV). My church had put this text to music and sang it frequently. When I suggested that it be sung at my wedding, the praise leader replied: "But that's not a wedding song," "It is now," I said. I could see her running the song through her mind before nodding in agreement.

Another strategy is to take time not only to pray but to be quiet and listen. Listen to the voice of God … that voice within that whispers directive words and thoughts. Or you may pick up an inspiring book that seems to have been specifically written with you in mind, or you might receive a text with a message that fits your specific situation. My mother was an avid reader of her Bible and spiritual literature. She wrote copious notes and kept them in books, papers, files, etc. It is uncanny, but invariably, in one of my limbo lows, one of those notes would pop out of a book, or an old letter drop out of a file, providing quick insight or the appropriate word of encouragement. This still occurs, even though she has long left this earth. Sometimes inspiration comes from a song you suddenly hear, or one that you yourself might well break out singing. As a child, I remember my loving, even-tempered grandmother always singing the hymn "Higher Ground."

"I'm pressing on the upward way,
New heights I'm gaining every day;
Still praying as I onward bound,
Lord, plant my feet on higher ground."[17]

Gramma would hum or mumble the other verses, but her voice would always ring loud and confident at the chorus:

"Lord, lift me up and let me stand,
By faith, on Heaven's table land;
A higher plane than I have found;
Lord, plant my feet on higher ground."[18]

Another strategy is to find someone to help. This approach must come from a prayerful exercise for the right person. Perhaps the most applicable biblical text when seeking spiritual aid can be found in Paul's letter to the Ephesians who were experiencing their own limbo lows because of his imprisonment. Ephesians 3:19–20:

"And to know the love of Christ, which passeth knowledge, that ye might be filled with all the fulness of God. Now unto him that is able to do exceeding abundantly above all that we ask or think, according to the power that worketh in us."

This text tends to draw our attention to a loving and powerful God, who will go beyond our wildest imagination to grant our requests. But we seldom focus on the second part of the text: **"according to the power that worketh in us."** It is one thing to know that you can receive from a loving and powerful Father far beyond what you can ask or think. It is another to understand fully that the result depends on the power that is working within you. In other words, the response to your request depends on the extent to which your battery is charged so that it could fully access the power within you.

Here are three serious questions:

1) Who are you when you are alone?
2) Who or what is powering you up?
3) Are you fully 100% charged?

---

17 "Higher Ground," Hymnary, https://1ref.us/wtw05.
18 Ibid.

What awesome power we must have, that this awesome, magnificent God, whom we have the privilege of calling Abba Father, can do exceedingly and abundantly above all that we ask or can even think. Yet it relies on the power that is working within us. So, to a large extent, it is on us. What kind of **POWER** is working in you?

This text in Paul's letter to the Ephesians has always tantalized me, because of the power it promises. It seems to speak of a power that's already in place, working in those of us who profess to be Christ-followers. More critically, it challenges us to utilize that power. Success really relies on the strength of our belief and hinges on the fact that we display our **belief** in the way we **behave**. Or to further clarify it, the way **we behave** indicates what we **believe.**

Our behavior is a grave responsibility because it points directly to our relationship with Jesus Christ, and it is through our relationship with Christ that we have the power to represent Him effectively. It begs the question: "Do you know Jesus, or do you only know about Him?" Quite a difference. It is to this knowledge of Jesus that our faith is tied. It must not be a faith that we could only mouth, but one we automatically live. How does our faith show up in challenging times, in the limbo lows that come when we are least expecting them?

During the second Obama election, I had worked hard as a volunteer. I felt I had sweat in the game, so I was praying just as hard. A few weeks before the election, I told my husband: "We got this. The Lord has told me he will win." I was strutting around with full confidence. On election night, the results were coming in from some of the highly Democratic states, and I remained confident. "Yes! Thank You, Jesus." And then results from the Republican states began to roll in, and my faith began to crumble. At one point, I didn't want to hear the television reports. I ran into the bathroom and locked myself up in terror. My husband was not letting me get away with it. "Aye, but I thought you told me the Lord said he will win. Where is your faith?"

Belief and behavior. How does our faith show up in challenging times when we need it most to counter those limbo lows?

Again, in his writings to the Ephesians with grace and peace as a special agent of Jesus Christ, Paul speaks about the connection between what we know about God, **how** we operationalize that knowledge, and **what** we do with that knowledge. If we truly believe, we will have completely submitted our lives to Him, and our behavior will be in perfect sync with God's plan and purpose for our lives. We will be confident that He will indeed go beyond our requests to fulfill His plans and purpose for our lives. In Isaiah 65:24 we are told:

> *"And it shall come to pass, that before they*
> *Call, I will answer; and while they are yet*
> *speaking, I will hear."*

Earlier in Ephesians 1:17, Paul had prayed that the *"God of our Lord Jesus Christ, the Father of glory, may give to you the spirit of wisdom and revelation in the knowledge of Him"* (NKJV). The purpose of this revelation is for a deeper knowledge and understanding that will deepen our experience with Christ. That is to say, a deeper and more personal relationship with Him. The death and resurrection of Christ removed the veil that separated sinful humanity from the Divinity. God wants to reveal Himself to us so that we can fully comprehend Him, partake of His awesome power, and use it; yes, in our own lives, but also in the lives of others as we win souls for Him. Again, the question remains: Do we really **KNOW** Christ, or do we just KNOW **about** HIM?

> *The question remains: Do we really **KNOW** Christ, or do we just KNOW **about** HIM?*

Paul's prayer for the Ephesians touches three areas which apply to our lives today, particularly in this moment of world history:

1. **First**, a full understanding of **why** He has called each one of us to be part of the body of Christ.

   "The eyes of your understanding being enlightened; that ye may know what is the hope of his calling, and what the riches of the glory of his inheritance in the saints" (Eph. 1:18).

   "And what is the exceeding greatness of his power to us-ward who believe, according to the working of his mighty power" (verse 19).

   We have to identify our **purpose and nurture its connection and reliance on that God power** *(verse 19)*.

2. **The second area** is a full understanding of the spiritual riches being passed to us through the life of Jesus Christ operating in others.

This means that our power can be recharged through the experiences of others. And more than that, we have a responsibility of helping to strengthen the belief in others by sharing our rich spiritual experiences. This is why it is so critical to share our testimonies with others.

3. **The third area** is a greater recognition of these spiritual riches and the power they represent in our lives. It is the only way we can strategically use them to activate the gifts and talents we have in order to empower us for His purpose. This is the connection between our purpose and our power. It is in fulfilling our purpose that we are fully empowered, our batteries 100% charged; green light on; ready to go. Action!

These three areas which Paul outlined point **to new spiritual growth** that will affect us personally and impact the lives of others. Our sin-sick world cries out for women and men fully functioning within the purpose for which they have been called and for which they have been empowered. It sends a special message for religious institutions to acknowledge the critical importance of women at this point in world history when serious attacks are being made to undermine and roll back the hard-earned rights of women.

The biblical representation of the church as "woman" is no accident. We have all been duly warned. Take heed!

*** *** ***

Guidance Text:
"For God hath not given us the spirit of fear; but of power, and of love, and of a sound mind" (2 Tim. 1:7).

CHAPTER 12

SPIRIT-FILLED AND FIRED UP

Conquering most of my limbo lows had been quite a testing period. Still, I had begun to think that my spiritual level was on a comfortable auto pilot. Then one Sunday at church, Pastor Sam preached a powerful Word from Acts, pointing to the absence of the Holy Spirit in our lives. I thought I had reached a spiritual height with my baptism, but apparently there was another level that I had not yet attained. Later I would discover that I was not unique in this regard. Many Christians operate at a level far beneath divine intention because we fail to accept and operationalize the most powerful gift received from our heavenly Father. Many religious institutions fail to guide their congregations in this direction, seeming to be afraid of the power of the Holy Spirit themselves.

In his extraordinary documentation of *The Black Church*, Professor Henry Louis Gates, Jr. writes of the complicated relationship Christians have with the Holy Spirit. "Possession is the 'language' through which God expresses God's self to the faithful, and 'unknown tongues' or 'speaking in tongues' is the 'language' in which the faithful respond to and communicate with God, and God alone, since no one else can translate."[19]

---

19 Henry Louis Gates, Jr., *The Black Church: This is Our Story, This is Our Song* (New York, NY: Penguin Press, 2021), p. 208.

Although there are many references to speaking in tongues in the Bible, this may well be alarming for many who are not Pentecostal or those who consider themselves full-gospel Christians. Gates writes about the "awe and condescension" often associated with the practice that many indeed consider a gift directly from the throne of God. And while many indeed find it "distasteful," "scary," and "disruptive," the infusion of the Holy Spirit, and the use of what Gates refers to as "the function of the Holy Ghost and its dazzling linguistic multiplicity,"[20] can well be considered a critical but underused gift, though it is linked to the promised "Comforter" (John 14:26).

To his credit, Pastor Sam was not fearful, but he was cautious. In his teachings, he had been careful to point out the Scriptures that insisted on the need to explain the messages of the Holy Spirit.

> ***"I would that ye all spake with tongues but rather that ye prophesied: for greater is he that prophesieth than he that speaketh with tongues, except he interpret, that the church may receive edifying" (1 Cor. 14:5).***

In fact, a young lady who was given to interrupting services with long spiritual utterances but failing to explain them to the congregation complained to me that Pastor Sam had asked her to stop unless they were accompanied by English explanations. She stopped. With that in mind, I returned to church one afternoon for a special seminar on the Holy Spirit.

The church was partly filled, but the sermon appeared to be a replica of a regular Sunday morning worship service. Pastor Sam gave a detailed explanation of the power of the Holy Spirit, and the need for His power (many believe the Holy Spirit is really female) in our lives. Using the spiritual prayer language was one way of ensuring total and complete guidance and empowerment by the Holy Spirit. When words fail us in our pleadings before the throne, the Holy Spirit would take our inadequate language and present them to the Lord. The Holy Spirit was our great interpreter. More critically, the Holy Spirit could present needs we couldn't even identify, or were loath to acknowledge, and present them to the Lord on our behalf.

That last explanation must have touched a nerve, because I found myself at the altar with other congregants seeking to be empowered by the Holy Spirit through the use of "tongues." With eyes tightly shut, I waited as Pastor Sam and two of the elders patiently prayed over each person. Did I

---

20 Ibid., p. 213.

doze off while standing? Because suddenly pastor's hand was on my forehead; he was anointing me with oil and telling me to open my mouth and say loudly whatever words came to my mind. I resisted and resisted, but they were patient. The three men prayed over me as Pastor Sam, with his kind, soothing voice, urged me to loudly speak the words that were at the tip of my tongue. After much prayer and pleading, unknown words came out of my mouth … first slowly and then with some rapidity. Pastor Sam urged me to continue to practice my new prayer language, and to expand on it as the Spirit leads. Shaken and shakily, I returned to my seat, convinced that there had been another major transformation in my life.

On the way home, I remembered my cousin, a born and well-bred Seventh-day Adventist, who had related a story of attending a Pentecostal church with two of her colleagues. During an intense prayer session, the colleague, who had invited them both and belonged to the church, began praying in the Spirit. At the end of the session, the other colleague turned to my cousin and whispered: "I didn't know she knew my language." He was from Africa, and their colleague was praying in a language that she did not even know, but her African invitee understood. I continued to use my new language in my prayer closet, particularly during those challenging life moments when I just did not know what to say or how to approach the Lord. Very often during the Sunday services, when there was an extra special need for corporate prayer, Pastor Sam would urge the congregation to "pray in the Spirit." I would use my new language but with some measure of shyness, though in corporate unison, we were each praying directly to God through the Holy Spirit, so there was no need for the required public explanation. While I continued to use my Spirit language in private prayer, there were long time gaps when I forgot or did not feel the need to use it. Imagine that … being given a powerfully useful gift yet not feeling the need to use it.

Paul is deliberate to point out that it is sin that brings about that gap between what we believe and how we behave. It is sin that causes the void between our purpose and our power. And it is the Holy Spirit that can bring those two areas together. The Holy Spirit is the force that stirs up the power in us. It brings us to a place of spiritual maturity, where there is a synergy between purpose and power. There is combined action that results in our behavior matching our belief. God has promised us this strength and overcoming power in order to accomplish the purpose for which He has sent us … as His representatives. As Christ-followers, we are indeed the priesthood of all believers.

Very often we limit God's wonder-working power in our lives. It is true for all of us, but it is a particular challenge for women because of the way in which we have been socialized, to follow, not to be so brazen as to lead. Thank God that is beginning to change as we see examples of women in positive leadership in so many areas. God is able to fulfill His purpose in our lives, and we can do ALL things through Christ who strengthens us (**Phil. 4:13**).

Jesus Christ was very careful to leave with us, "the Comforter," aka the Holy Spirit. We have within us the same Spirit that raised Christ from the dead! That is a powerful thought. We should be laying hands on the sick and seeing rapid improvement; the words coming out of our mouths should overturn doubt and shyness and bind the evil forces that attack us and those we love. We should be walking in a Spirit of holy boldness. We have lying within us the Spirit to make the devil tremble when we get up in the morning. Our very presence should repel the enemy so we can shine the light that brings others to Jesus. We should be binding with all our spiritual power the violence pervading our social and political environment. But so many of us are plagued with the spirit of fear. Fear is a wicked and demonic spirit. But the text from 2 Timothy 1:7, another of my road marches, reminds us: **"For God hath not given us the spirit of fear; but of power, and of love, and of a sound mind."**

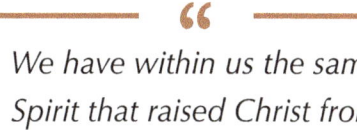

> *We have within us the same Spirit that raised Christ from the dead!*

These are the forces we have to stir up within us. We have to tear down the strongholds in our lives to reveal our true power. Strongholds of fear. Doubt. Anger. Resentment. Unforgiveness. Jealousy. Feelings of inadequacy. So let us take the time to note how the Spirit is moving in our lives. In fact, we should be deliberate about praying for the presence of the Holy Spirit in our lives to make us aware of our purpose and to identify and focus on the gifts and talents we are gifted in order to become more involved and effective. We should be actively praying to stir up and utilise the hidden gifts within us.

There are five things we need to stir up the power working for us…

1. The **Holy Spirit**: Jesus Christ clearly promised to leave us with the Holy Spirit: **"I will pray the Father, and he shall give you another Comforter, that he may abide with you for ever,"** He said (John

14:16). We are all carrying within us this awesome power, yet it seems we are hesitant to use it. The Holy Spirit is our helper, our Comforter. Our advocate. Our guide. In **John 14:12-14**, Jesus promises:

> *"Verily, verily, I say unto you, He that believeth on me, the works that I do shall he do also; and greater works than these shall he do; because I go unto my Father. And whatsoever ye shall ask in my name, that will I do, that the Father may be glorified in the Son. If ye shall ask any thing in my name, I will do it."*

It is a powerful promise that we should all draw on.

2. **Love**. It is clearly the most powerful force in the universe. God so loves us, with all of our sinful and human frailties, that He sent His Son to die for us, then left us a Comforter and Protector.

   In one of the best examples of His overwhelming love, He sent the Comforter: *John 14:26-27:*

   > *"But the Comforter, which is the Holy Ghost, whom the Father will send in my name, he shall teach you all things, and bring all things to your remembrance, whatsoever I have said unto you. Peace I leave with you, my peace I give unto you: not as the world giveth, give I unto you. Let not your heart be troubled, neither let it be afraid."*

How can we not strive to pass on that love to others ... sometimes even to the seemingly most unlovable? We are living at a time and in an environment of hate, in a world that is laden with hate and division. We will be challenged to show God's love in many ways. May God help us all!

3. **Knowledge.** God has blessed us with a love letter, the Bible, so we can know Him and prove His love, concern, and guidance. We have to stay in **the Word**, so we can crush the enemy with the powerful promises in the Bible when we are filled with thoughts of doubt and fear, when our battery is running low. The psalmist reminds us that *"Thy word is a lamp unto my feet, and a light unto my path"* (**Ps. 119:105**). Our Father has provided a means for us to constantly communicate with Him through *prayer*. You know the drill. "Little prayer, little power; much prayer, much power."

4. **Faith**. The faith chapter, Hebrews 11, tells us that "without faith it is impossible to please [God]" (verse 6). It also tells us that *we must walk by faith, not by sight* (2 Cor. 5:7, paraphrase). Through faith in God, our spiritual eyes will be opened so we can see, feel, and throw into full gear God's supernatural intervention in our own life and the lives of others.
5. **Recall**: We have to remember and recall the many ways in which the Lord has saved us, picked us up, dusted us off, turned us around, protected us, provided for us, sustained us, and equipped us to fulfill the purpose for which He has prepared us. We have to first tell these stories to ourselves and stir up the power within us. We have to tell each other these stories to encourage each other. We have to tell our children these stories so they will know how we overcame adversities. That is the **pow**er that is working with us that we must continue to stir up, nurture, and activate. As I'm sure you check your phone several times a day to make sure your battery is **ALWAYS** 100% charged, do the same to make sure you have enough spiritual juice that will enable you to function powerfully.

> *As I'm sure you check your phone several times a day to make sure your battery is ALWAYS 100% charged, do the same to make sure you have enough spiritual juice that will enable you to function powerfully.*

May God fill us all with His grace, favour, and the Holy Spirit to boldly tap into the power that He has given us to accomplish His purpose in our lives.

*** *** ***

Guidance Text:
"But as it is written, Eye hath not seen, nor ear heard, neither have entered into the heart of man, the things which God hath prepared for them that love him. But God hath revealed them unto us by his Spirit: for the Spirit searcheth all things, yea, the deep things of God" (1 Cor. 2:9–10).

CHAPTER 13

LESSONS FROM MY GARDEN

It is no accident that two major events in human history took place in gardens: the fall of humanity in the Garden of Eden and the breakthrough of redemption in the Garden of Gethsemane. Gardens are tremendous sites of revelation and revival. Gardening is a powerful, though often underestimated, strategy for recharging your battery. Seeing the divine imprint on the shapes and colours of flowers, vegetables, trees, the tiny moving creatures, buzzing with life that pop up in a spade full of earth is a stark affirmation of creation and the Creator.

In preparation for the COVID lockdown, I decided to sharpen my gardening interests. No, I'm not one of those true-true, experienced gardeners. I'm really a newbie. But my intention to take gardening more seriously took me on an introductory tour of my own garden … or what passed for a garden. What began as an opportunity to evaluate became a serious time to remember … to recall … to reflect.

My first and almost hilarious reflection was on my attempt to plant one of my favourite flowers, the hydrangea, at the side of our then home in

Maryland. I had been thrilled to see the plants turn from tiny shrubs into the huge leaves of the hydrangea that I could recognize. One day, while clearing the persistent weeds from around the hydrangea plants, I saw a new leaf that looked strangely familiar. I decided to allow it to grow a bit longer before clearing it as one of those pushy weeds. As the leaf grew into a more recognizable plant, I remembered my sister, on a recent visit, had brought some pumpkins (aka Calabaza squash) for the preparation of our native Trini callaloo dish. I had casually thrown the pumpkin seeds at the side of the house, even before planting the hydrangeas. Knowing full well that pumpkins would be challenged by Maryland's wintry months, I had not given the act a second thought. But the seeds haphazardly thrown there were determined. Their leaves continued to grow bigger, to bend and swerve into a vine, and to skillfully and stubbornly wind around my hydrangeas. Then they threw out glorious yellow buds that slowly expanded before shaping themselves into tiny recognizable pumpkins that grew and grew and grew, in both size and number. When the oldest pumpkin grew so large as though it would burst, and the colour of the skin showed signs of turning from green to amber, I harvested it in wild delirium, and had to get

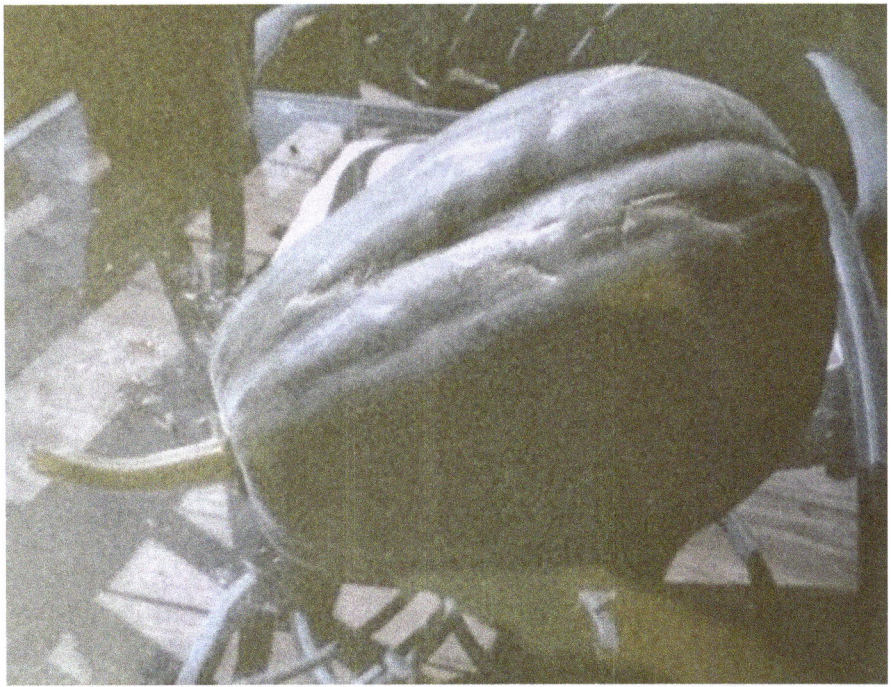

One of the miracle pumpkins, harvested from the planting of hydrangeas.

help lugging it into the house. After cutting it into several pieces, I shared that miracle pumpkin with several friends, who celebrated with me the miraculous blessing of planting hydrangeas and reaping pumpkins.

Central to understanding the whole experience were the lessons of divine **guidance, gratitude, and provision,** underscored by the additional lesson of the importance of sharing one's blessings. But there were two additional lessons still to come. Shortly after my miracle harvest, I visited my former Agape Ministries Church on a return trip to Trinidad. Late, as usual, I entered through the back entrance, only to find a storeroom overflowing with the largest, healthiest pumpkins I had ever seen. I was later told that there had been such a bountiful harvest of pumpkins that year, that members were bringing in their pumpkins, begging others to take enough to distribute to friends and neighbours outside the church. That was the first lesson of **overflowing blessings** that ignore distance. Blessings that acknowledged my connection with the church and reached me all the way in Maryland, USA. Hallelujah!

A related lesson is the power of **intercessory prayer**. Apparently, the church had kept me on their prayer list, sending up prayers so powerful that they transcended time and space, without the need for a passport or airline ticket. Double hallelujah! Perhaps it is for this specific purpose that the Bible advises us to forsake not the gathering of the saints. This is indeed an instructive guide to post-COVID worshippers who are content with having a spiritual relationship with God yet do not feel it necessary to physically attend a church. The fact remains that belonging to a church family ensures the constant prayerful support and encouragement that are too powerful to ignore or forsake.

In the business of life, we rarely have time to pause to reflect. It is a particularly important habit to acquire now, as time and indeed people are passing so quickly before our eyes. Many of us have lost loved ones. We are surrounded by so much sorrow, sadness, and struggles. It occurred to me that a big plan of the COVID-19 pandemic was not only to kill, separate, or keep people lonely and depressed. A major strategy was and continues to be to steal our joy. So, let us seriously consider **JOY**—the joy of gardening, but also the true **JOY** that comes from the throne room itself. The Bible tells us that weeping and mourning will endure for a night, but **JOY** comes in the morning (Ps. 30:5). The text brings to mind the tiny purple flower aptly called "morning glory" that salutes the morning with the beauty that surrounds us, allowing us to see and to be awed by the glory of a loving Father. Oh, if we could only take the time to hit pause amid all our busyness and open our hearts and minds so that we might truly see the beauty and the joy that we have been gifted, both in the natural and the spiritual, particularly in these perilous times.

These morning glory reflections took me back to when my husband Tony and I first moved to Florida and hired a Cuban landscaper to help. He was assessing the garden and pointing to things that had to be trimmed, transplanted, and re-planted or rooted out and discarded. There was one scraggly root, which I knew for sure would be added to the throw-out heap. Instead, he exclaimed with much excitement: "*Mira! Mira! Usted tiene una Tabebuia. Es una Tabebuia.* [You have Tabebuia. It's a Tabebuia.]" I had no idea what that was, but he was the expert, so I figured he knew what he was talking about, and I was impressed with his excitement to have found it. To my surprise he said, "We'll put it over here, because it needs much space to grow." He rooted up the stringy shrub and located a spot on our limited space for this mysterious Tabebuia. The stringy plant did begin to grow and fill out slowly but not rapidly enough to make any real impression. Then my florist friend, Jen, visited one day, and she, too, was thrilled: "Oh, you have a Tabebuia." Now Jen has encyclopedic knowledge of and about every growing flower known to woman and man. "It has shallow roots, so don't let it grow too tall," she warned. *This Tabebuia must be something special*, I thought. Still, I remained unimpressed.

The next spring as we began to become familiar with Florida, I noticed and admired these huge trees with beautiful bunches of golden yellow flowers. *How I would love to have one of those trees*, I thought. Then one day my scraggly tree began to throw out a few clusters of those same bright yellow, trumpet-shaped flowers. Only then did I realise that this Tabebuia tree was the plant I had been admiring all over Florida. That brought immense joy. But something else clicked. There was something I was missing about this rescue plant. Something about this flower struck a chord within me, not unlike the feeling you get when you meet someone whose face is familiar … and then you realise it's either a cousin or someone with whom you had grown up a long time ago or with whom you had gone to school. I decided to consult Uncle Google, who was quick to explain: "Commonly known as the 'Golden Trumpet Tree, Tabebuia, or the Poui, as it is known in Trinidad, is one of the most beautiful flowering trees that can be seen in Trinidad and Tobago.'"

What! But Uncle Google was not done: "Did you know that the Yellow Poui is native to Trinidad and Tobago?"

The Poui (Tabebuia) in full bloom. Photo by Gwen Mitchell.

Now in Trinidad and Tobago, in addition to the steelpan,[21] which was invented there, and the calypso, the Poui tree is a major cultural fixture. Once a year, the yellow Poui turns the hills of the northern and southern ranges into fields of golden blossoms, and every Trini school child can tell you that the flowering of the Poui signals the end of the dry season and the beginning of the rainy season, the time for farmers to begin to plant. It has always been one of my favourite trees, but because it grows primarily in the mountains, I had always admired it from afar. The thought that there was a Poui tree planted in my postage stamp garden, already planted before I got there, was beyond every flight of fantasy. This is the awesome God we serve. God, with His extravagant and eternal love, long before we had even thought of moving to Florida, had placed this Poui tree for me … with its

---

21   *The steelpan was invented in Trinidad & Tobago in the 1930s. Its history has been traced to the resistance against the enslavement of Africans in Trinidad. Steelpan production and playing technique have spread throughout the Caribbean and the world. In 2023, the United Nations declared August 11 as World Steelpan Day.*

fancy, botanical name, Tabebuia ... that I, in my ignorance, did not even recognise. It is no exaggeration that He knows our names; He knows every hair on our heads. He knows our nature. He created us, so He knows what brings us that indescribable JOY.

The enemy has a full-time occupation to steal our joy, and we have to be intentional about fighting against it. In the middle of all of the sadness, sorrow, doubt, uncertainty, understandable depression, and often panic about the pandemic, the violence, the racism ... in the midst of the horror of George Floyd's public, torturous murder; in the midst of the assault on our senses as we see and hear the continuing weekly police violence against Black, Brown and Asian peoples, let's make it a point to stop, look, and SEE! Let's take the time to ENJOY the joys that the Lord has put in our path to give us strength, even in the midst of our earthly trials. Let's look, see, recognise, and acknowledge His glory.

Indeed, it had not even entered my mind that our loving Father would organise a Poui tree in my front yard, years before we got there, His goodness running ahead of us. God has said in His Word that before you call, He will answer, and while you are yet speaking, He will hear (Isa. 65:24). He knows you. He knows what's troubling you. He knows your fears and your anxieties, your weakness, and your strengths. He knows what makes you happy. And He has gone out of His way to prepare a place for you. Not only in heaven, as He promised, but here on earth, to help us in our earthly struggles ... if only we will take the time to look and build a memory bank. This certainly points to the importance of journaling.

For years I wrote, nightly, a "Thank You" journal that documented not only answered prayers, but simple, everyday moments of joy. It is a way of reminding us that we serve an awesome God. He is an unchanging God who placed a colourful ribbon in the sky to remind us of His continuing love and to give us hope. With that same awesome and excess love, He gave us the plan of salvation. He gave His only begotten Son for sinful us and sent Him to exhibit His love for the poor, the marginalized, and dispossessed in a way the world is still struggling to understand and interpret. Excess love. Examples of His love and caring reign in the beauty that lies around us, if we could just press pause on our worry and fear to focus on His goodness.

Mathew 6:28–30 documents Jesus' invitation to:

> *"Consider the lilies of the field, how they grow; they toil not, neither do they spin: And yet I say unto you, That even Solomon in*

all his glory was not arrayed like one of these. Wherefore, if God so clothe the grass of the field, which to day is, and to morrow is cast into the oven, shall he not much more clothe you, O ye of little faith?"

Interestingly, the white lilies, which are used primarily at the so-called Easter[22] weekend to symbolize the resurrection, represent rebirth and hope and are often referred to as "white robed apostles of hope." Undeniably, the text, also reported by Dr. Luke, in **chapter 12:27**, speaks of God's divine love, care, and the beauty which He has carefully created for us. The lilies have a trumpet shape similar to the golden trumpets of the Poui that, like the lilies, sound the message, not only that it is the end of the dry season and the beginning of the rainy season but a symbolic cleansing that washes away the filth of worldly sin. What a symbol of HOPE!

And in **verse 33** of Matthew 6, Jesus advises us:

"But seek ye first the kingdom of God, and his righteousness; and all these things shall be added unto you."

Surely this is an early identification of the need to seek divine guidance as the key that unlocks the path to successful earthly lives in our journey. Jesus commands us to tear down the strongholds in our lives so we could experience, taste, and see His joy, His grace, His beauty. It is in the Garden of Gethsemane that Jesus underwent the agony of His imminent death, where He prayed on the night of His betrayal and arrest, the night before His crucifixion. From there He removed the obstacle of sin and provided the breakthrough of redemption.

Our peace and our joy have been purchased by the precious blood of Jesus. Remembering, recalling, and reflecting on this is critical to our ability to survive, to thrive, and especially to spread the news in these end times. This awesome love is not for us to keep for ourselves. Our task is to be proactive in spreading it far and wide, especially to the unlovable. People recognize and carefully observe Christ-followers. Whether you know it or not, whether they admit it or not, people are famished for direction; they are looking at you for guidance. In this era of hate, when our ability to love is always being challenged, we are to clothe ourselves in this **peace** and model the **joy** that comes from knowing and following Christ. This is the most effective outreach or evangelism tool.

---

22 Christ-followers now prefer the term Resurrection Weekend to diminish its association with egg hunts and bunny rabbits, as fun as they might be.

Knowing that His disciples would need something to sustain them in the struggles after He ascended, Jesus assured us of victory, through His peace.

> *"These things I have spoken unto you, that in me ye might have peace. In the world ye shall have tribulation: but be of good cheer; I have overcome the world" (John 16:33).*

Our Creator of incredible beauty expects us to enjoy that beauty and the peace that it brings. In speaking through Isaiah in **chapter 55:12** we are urged to walk confidently:

> *"Go out with joy, and be led forth with peace: the mountains and the hills shall break forth before you into singing, and all the trees of the field shall clap their hands."*

Our magnificent God not only deals in Tabebuia or Poui trees. He is even more dramatic and direct … and always on time. Years ago, on May 25, 2021, to be exact, He had seeded and planted in the square, where George Floyd was tortured to death, a disparate group of angels. A "bouquet of humanity," one of the prosecuting attorneys called them. Young as they were, they all must have been rushed to the spot on emergency wings, so they had no time to don their angelic robes. One such angel, a mere seventeen-year-old teenager in blue jeans, a hoodie, and flip-flops, had cause to whip out her smartphone. With a steady hand for almost ten minutes, she videotaped the horror that was playing out before her eyes. Doubtlessly guided by the Holy Spirit, she posted the video clip online in what became a viral post that turned upside down the official explanation that the police department had already released. The outcome of that teenage action continues to have a significant, transformative effect on violence and particularly police violence, not only in the US, but throughout the world. What an example of our God in action, setting the stage long before, to put Darnella Frazier in place to accomplish His purpose. Hallelujah!

Moreover, our God is broad and dramatic in His action. The Floyd family had been nurtured by a praying mother. This huge family had descended on Minneapolis from all over the country to support each other. They held hands and prayed EVERY morning of the trial. Then, in the televised response to the verdict, they held hands, prayed, and gave thanks and praises to almighty God … FOR THE ENTIRE WORLD TO SEE AND HEAR. HALLELUJAH. What a witness! In the midst of their suffering,

God showed up to reveal Himself and His mighty and everlasting love in a powerful way! Indeed the Lord promises *in Jeremiah 31:12–13 (NKJV).*

> *Their souls shall be like a well-watered garden,*
> *And they shall sorrow no more at all.*
> *Then shall the virgin rejoice in the dance,*
> *And the young men and the old, together;*
> *For I will turn their mourning to joy,*
> *Will comfort them,*
> *And make them rejoice rather than sorrow.*

> *Friends, we need to stop, look, and pay attention to what the divine power is doing around us.*

Friends, we need to stop, look, and pay attention to what the divine power is doing around us. His mercies are all around us. We are in the End-times, and things are happening fast. The final movements are rapid ones. But His Glory is all around us, and His messages of comfort, encouragement, and hope are clear:

- **Ps. 37:4, "Delight thyself also in the LORD: and he shall give thee the desires of thine heart."**
- **Ps. 91:7, "A thousand shall fall at thy side, and ten thousand at thy right hand; but it shall not come nigh thee."**
- **Ps. 23:5–6, "Thou preparest a table before me in the presence of mine enemies: thou anointest my head with oil; my cup runneth over. Surely goodness and mercy shall follow me all the days of my life: and I will dwell in the house of the LORD for ever."**

Hence we must:

Recall … God's Favour

Remember … God's Promises

Reflect … on His Goodness

Revel … in His Glory

Remember that before Jesus ascended to heaven, He prayed a special prayer to His Father just for you and me.

John 17:22-24:

And the glory which thou gavest me I have given them; that they may be one, even as we are one: I in them, and thou in me, that they may be made perfect in one; and that the world may know that thou hast sent me, and hast loved them, as thou hast loved me. Father, I will that they also, whom thou hast given me, be with me where I am; that they may behold my glory, which thou hast given me: for thou lovedst me before the foundation of the world.

It is this glory that comes from being one in Christ that we are challenged to behold so that we could in turn be His link to others (the "godless," as the Message Bible says). But this glory can only come from the peace and joy that we Christ-followers find within our hearts; the peace and love that will overflow into our homes, our neighbourhoods, our church, our workplaces. It is this glory that we receive every morning … the Morning Glory … if we would only take the time to linger … to recall … to remember … to reflect … to count His many blessings and His overflowing goodness to us. For He has promised:

"I will never leave you nor forsake you" (Heb. 13:5, NKJV).
And in **Joshua 1:9:**

"Have I not commanded thee? Be strong and of a good courage; be not afraid, neither be thou dismayed: for the LORD, THY God is with thee whithersoever thou goest."

*** *** ***

Guidance Text:
"But as it is written, Eye hath not seen, nor ear heard, neither have entered into the heart of man, the things which God hath prepared for them that love him" (1 Cor. 2:9).
HALLELUJAH!!!

CHAPTER 14

THE INSURRECTION VS. THE RESURRECTION

"Truth shall spring out of the earth," says David in Psalm 85:11. As usual, it is made even clearer in the Message Bible: "Truth sprouts green from the ground." The search for truth became a critical issue for me as religion and politics merged into a scary, divisive mess. Its link to Satan, the father of lies (John 8:44), was and remains unmistakable and bears a nagging concern. Which side should a Christ-follower take? The side of disinformation, destruction, and physical and spiritual death? Or the side of grace and truth, redemption, hope, and a victorious life? The side of the insurrection? Or the side of resurrection, with its hope and promise of eternal life? It is our choice ... our decision ... our life. Both our physical and spiritual lives.

Such ruminations begged for a garden stroll to examine a crepe myrtle I had planted in my front garden. As a relatively new gardener, I had forgotten all about the plant, but there it was, in a struggle for life. It had been a gift from one of my "green thumb" cousins. I was sure she would one day ask about its survival, so I set out to look for it. After much searching, I found the crepe myrtle plant intertwined in a white jasmine bush that had completely embraced the plant in a deadly hug. The leaves of both plants were so similar; they were indistinguishable, a lesson in itself. Only careful examination could reveal the red vein that God had sneaked into the leaf of the crepe myrtle to distinguish it from the wily jasmine.

After a lengthy consultation, Carlos, the faithful gardener, cut the jasmine back down to the root. He assured me that cutting back the new growth several times would force the jasmine to give up and die, freeing the crepe myrtle to thrive. But after several repeats of that exercise, it was clear that the stubborn jasmine was taking no guidance from Carlos. It continued to grow, stifling the crepe myrtle. One day, in total exasperation, I suggested that we root up both plants, destroy the unwanted jasmine, release the roots of the crepe myrtle, then replant it. Carlos did not agree.

"It will die," he countered.

"It's dying now," I argued. "Let's give it a try."

Days later I watched the tiny crepe myrtle wither into a mere stick. Still, I watered it. I talked to it. Yes, I prayed over it. A few weeks later, a tiny stalk pushed through the earth. I thought it was another of those pushy weeds, but I was hopeful. Two weeks later, two more stalks with tiny leaves stuck out confidently in different directions … definite signs of new growth. Day by day, the stalks grew taller and taller into healthy wayward branches. The following spring, the still-small tree displayed its first crepe myrtle blossoms. Sparse blossoms, but for me it was a major victory as well as a dramatic visualization of the way in which truth and lies, good and evil, grow up together, intertwined, the one wrapping itself around the other until one is stifled to death. I was witnessing similar examples unfold in real life.

Lying has been central to human history. "Lie language," the Message Bible dubs it in its paraphrasing of **Psalm 12**. It began in the Garden of Eden, Satan directly contradicting God's word by telling Eve: "Ye shall not surely die" (Gen. 3:4). Lying has progressed throughout the centuries on personal levels, in historical documentation, political discourse, governmental policies, and religious proclamations and interpretations. The United States has been bombarded with the big political, electoral lie that has continued to divide and destroy personal, business, and government relations and to threaten its democratic governance.

Still, there is another big fat lie from the pit of hell. That is the lie of race. There is no such thing as race. Race is an artificial social construct. Neither biology nor any other branch of science supports this demonic idea. Yet the concept of race has been carefully and demonically created and designed to divide and conquer the human population. **There is one race: the human race, with all of its awesome diversity.** How I wish people would cease using the bogus, devilish, and divisive concept of race. But a human hierarchy has been carefully crafted to justify and normalize the exploitation of people based on this artificial construction: "race." There is, however, racism in all its myriad incarnations, strategically used to redefine, divide, and conquer ethnicities for continued exploitation. According to James Cone:

> Racism is a disease that perverts one's moral sensitivity and distorts the intellect. It is found not only in American society and its churches but particularly in the discipline of theology, affecting its nature and purpose."[23]

More wickedly, the concept of "race" has been used to ensure that those divisions are baked into a multilayered cake of conflict, confusion, exploitation, and inequality.

Scientists have long declared that humans share more than 99.9 percent of our DNA, making us all almost identical. Physical differences have been linked to environment, social differences, and cultural conditioning. According to Pulitzer Prize winning author, Isabel Wilkerson, in her outstanding bestseller, *Caste*, race is "a fiction told by modern humans for so long that it has come to be seen as a sacred truth."[24]

In recent pre- and post-COVID history, though, we have experienced lying at such high levels and with such rapidity and intensity that new words and phrases have been formed around it: "disinformation," "spinning," "gaslighting," "false equivalency," "framing the narrative," and "the weaponization of language." At the end of a statement, young people have taken to adding: "for real," in full understanding of the fantasy land in which they have been forced to exist. One writer refers to it as "the Age of Disinformation." As if in response to deliberate efforts to explain the struggle and protect unity, a whole new culture has arisen: wokeism. Wokeism is a concept crafted to warn African Americans and other oppressed groups to literally keep your eyes open; to stay awake; to be aware; to stay informed; to understand; to unravel your own reality in order to successfully navigate it … and, more critically, to stay alive. But that, too, has been co-opted and strategically misinterpreted for political gains, and more viciously as a tool to bludgeon African Americans and to undermine and eradicate Black history.

---

23 James Cone, *A Black Theology of Liberation* (Maryknoll, NY: Orbis Books, 1986), p. xxii.
24 Isabel Wilkerson, *Caste: The Origins of Our Discontents* (New York, NY: Random House, 2020), p. 66.

At the beginning of the year 2021, January 6 to be exact, a whole new level of lying was ushered in with the storming of the Capitol, the seat of government in Washington, D.C. As the cycle of lying often goes, the event was organised to uphold another lie, that of a stolen election in the United States … a lie that ties back to the racism birthed in the belly of the initial lie of race. Most of us witnessed it with our own eyes as though it were an afternoon television horror story, scheduled too early for children. Then the horror was multiplied as we heard it described as a "picnic." Insurrectionists have been described as "tourists," and although we heard the shots that resulted in the killing of one person, and saw the beating of several, the then president referred to it as a love fest. "Love was in the air," he said. Should I believe my lying ears?

What followed has been the acceleration and amazing flurry of lies, accompanied by the seeming normalization that gave rise to increased domestic terrorism, white supremacy, and the self-revelation of Christian nationalists. The incoming US President Biden warned that white supremacy was the nation's "most dangerous threat." But the Bible, always on point, nailed it in its comment on lies in **John 8:44** that introduced us to the father of lies: Satan.

"Ye are of your father the devil, and the lusts of your father ye will do. He was a murderer from the beginning, and abode not in the truth, because there is no truth in him. When he speaketh a lie, he speaketh of his own: for he is a liar, and the father of it."

Satan has been a liar and a murderer from the very beginning. And he has been wielding this major weapon to lie, to deceive and separate people from each other, on one hand; and to cause suicide—and indirectly homicide—when one considers the lies that accompanied the COVID vaccines which saved many lives. In His warning about events before His Second Coming, Jesus says:

"For false Christs and false prophets will arise and will show great signs and wonders, so as to mislead, if possible, even the very elect" **(Matt. 24:24).**

It is even more disturbing that so much of the fearmongering and confusion about the COVID vaccine was being spread by churches. And because of the power of the American media, this confusion had been transported to the Caribbean, where churches were spreading fear as people were dying. Governments trying to protect their citizens were met with heavy criticism. There were violent protests in Antigua and Barbuda and

Guadeloupe; in St. Vincent, the prime minister was stoned ... all of this as the virus spread its death and destruction.

Needless to say, these issues caused me to revisit and review all the doubts, questions, and concerns I had about organised religion and some of the contradictions I had experienced, including those related to ethnicity and gender. It became very clear that emphasis must be placed on a personal relationship with God, not religion. While the Bible certainly advises that we "not [forsake] assembling" **(Heb. 10:25, NKJV)**, it is of paramount importance that we develop a relationship with God, through His Son, Jesus, and take direction and guidance directly from God, through the Holy Spirit.

The question arises: How are we Christ-followers to respond in this period of lying, confusion, and chaos? How do we navigate the distrust and destruction that it has brought? Informed care and caution must be taken to identify and extricate truth from lies and to nurture the truth thoughtfully and prayerfully. As we pray for protection for ourselves and others, we must pray for wisdom ... the wisdom to make wise choices. Choices that will help, not harm us. Remember it is God who created science and gave humans—women and men—the knowledge to create vaccines. ***James 1:5*** provides the assurance *that* if we need wisdom, we should ask our generous God, who will not only grant it, but will do so liberally and without reproach.

We are told that the last day movements will be rapid, and we are already experiencing unprecedented fires, floods, hurricanes, volcanoes, not to mention the horrors of war. We will be forced to make many life and death decisions. Thankfully, we can rely on the protection of an all-powerful God. It warms my heart when in the Old Testament books of Numbers and Deuteronomy God repeatedly identifies Himself as: "God, Your God." He repeatedly reminds us of His power and the fact that He belongs to us. We have this mighty power operating within us on which to draw. Our guidance text provides further assurance:

John 14:13–18:

And whatsoever ye shall ask in my name, that will I do, that the Father may be glorified in the Son. If ye shall ask any thing in my name, I will do it. If ye love me, keep my commandments. And I will pray the Father, and he shall give you another Comforter, that he may abide with you for ever; Even the Spirit of truth; whom the world cannot receive, because it seeth him not, neither knoweth him: but ye know him; for he dwelleth with you, and shall be in you. I will not leave you comfortless: I will come to you.

It is the infusion of the Holy Spirit that is our hope in the resurrection, as opposed to the violence, death, and destruction of the insurrection and all it represents. The resurrection represents life. Everlasting life. My prayer is that God will guide us all to choose Him, and that we will remain committed, equipped, and ready in the end-time battle and its numerous fronts. That battle has already been won. Thank You, Jesus!

*** *** ***

Guidance Text:
"Trust in the Lord with all thine heart; and lean not unto thine own understanding. In all thy ways acknowledge him, and he shall direct thy paths" (Prov. 3:5–6).

CHAPTER 15

ONE LITTLE LIGHT

Without a doubt there were many periods of my life when my faith needed a good spicing up. Reflections took me to a Scripture class at the convent high school I attended in Trinidad. In her exegesis on the text in Matthew 5:13 that refers to Christ-followers as "the salt of the earth," Mother Eugenia, one of the few local nuns teaching the class, joked that the Lord had specifically made salt for eggs, tomatoes, and *zaboca*, the word used for avocado in Trinidad, transposed from the Aztec name *ahuacatl*. "Could you imagine how those things would taste without salt?" she asked.

Salt is indeed a preservative in societies without refrigeration, and so it was a very valuable commodity. It is also used for flavouring, to add spice and interest to foods, which is exactly what we, as Christ-followers, are expected to be … a valuable, preserving, and enhancing presence to influence those with whom we come in contact. It is a call to intermingle with the world and help to transform it by our very presence. If the salt loses its flavor, if we lose our way, if we lose or dilute the message we have, we are worthless to influence those with whom we come in contact. *Ouch!* The text, as applied to Christ-followers, speaks to the seasoning, marinating, spicing up of our faith so that we can accomplish His purpose.

Along with salt is the power of light. Have you ever noticed how winged insects are attracted to light? In my house, I am considered the Fly Ninja. I go crazy when I see a fly; I have devised an effective fly-killing strategy. The first thing I do is arm myself with insect spray and somehow get the winged intruder to a window, through which light is streaming. When the fly settles there, s/he is history. That is an example of the magnetic power of light. Both salt and light are active forces that change situations and environments, adding good flavor to our families, friends, and by extension, our community.

In the Sermon on the Mount, Jesus spoke of the power of light, His light, to draw others to Him. The audience was made up of His disciples but also a wider group of people: His potential followers. Jesus warned that Christ-followers will be reviled and persecuted, but in the face of that He said:

> *"Rejoice, and be exceeding glad: for great is your reward in heaven: for so persecuted they the prophets which were before you" (Matt. 5:12).*

It is the "CliffsNotes," as students would say, for the prescription for righteous living as divine grace. Jesus acknowledges the powers of salt and light and uses these concepts to help us to understand the spiritual impact we are to have on those around us, in spite of the many challenges.

> *"Ye are the salt of the earth: but if the salt have lost his savour, wherewith shall it be salted? It is thenceforth good for nothing, but to be cast out, and to be trodden under foot of men" (Matt. 5:13).*

Light symbolizes awareness, knowledge, and understanding. It also symbolizes direction … readiness for a journey. In summary, Jesus put His stamp on us and gave us the road map and His marching orders.

> *"Ye are the light of the world. A city that is set on an hill cannot be hid. Neither do men light a candle, and put it under a bushel, but on a candlestick; and it giveth light unto all that are in the house. Let your light so shine before men, that they may see your good works, and glorify your Father which is in heaven" (Matt. 5:14–16).*

So what are our marching orders as Christ-followers? It is not to retreat but to **engage**. **Engagement** is an important role to play, particularly in a world that is becoming even more challenging. A recent study revealed that the rate of "anxiety and depression increased by a massive 25%."[25] "Ninety-percent of U.S. adults [believe] that the country is facing a mental health crisis, according to a recent KFF/CNN survey."[26] Since the coronavirus pandemic, not only have mental health issues become more common, but the world has become even more dangerous socially, economically, politically, and yes, spiritually. How then do we spread love and shine His light in a climate of heightened racism and xenophobia? In an environment of increasing hostility and violence? In the mainstreaming of lies? In a time when disinformation has begun to sabotage not only Black history but government and even attempting to reinterpret the Word?

Our role is not only to prepare ourselves and to pray for ourselves but to represent ... to do good for others, to help prepare others, to pray for others, to shine a light, His light.

Remember, He said:

"I am the light of the world. Whoever follows me will not walk in darkness, but will have the light of life" (John 8:12, ESV).

In other words, Jesus is saying to us, His followers, "Just as I shone, now I want you to shine." It sets the standard for us to follow. It is, indeed, a tremendous responsibility, but it does not do much good if we have the light but are negligent about shining it.

The question becomes: Are we fully embracing His light? Are we shining His light? If not, what kind of light are we shining? The Scripture explains:

"Take no part in the unfruitful works of darkness, but instead expose them. For it is shameful even to speak of the things that they do in secret" (Eph. 5:11–12, ESV).

The text points to the need to be intentional about doing good in these evil days. The Sermon on the Mount tells us how we are to live once we are made right with God ... how to live our lives by simply doing good in the world. You can't just talk the light. You have to walk it. You have to let it shine to illuminate your surroundings. Indeed, the light reminds us of His majesty, His victory, and the hope He represents but also that we can

---

25 "COVID-19 pandemic triggers 25% increase in prevalence of anxiety and depression worldwide," World Health Organization, published March 2, 2022, https://1ref.us/wtw06.
26 "The Implications of COVID-19 for Mental Health and Substance Use," KFF, published March 20, 2023, https://1ref.us/wtw07.

be a blessing to others. His light is not just about us. He wants us to have a visible presence ... to be that city on the hill: **Verse 14–15**:

> *"Ye are the light of the world. A city that is set on an hill cannot be hid. Neither do men light a candle, and put it under a bushel, but on a candlestick; and it giveth light unto all that are in the house."*

The first place to let your light shine is in your home. In your house. The Christian light must first shine in your home so it can radiate out on others. One of the many tributes to the departed Colin Powell described him as a bright "point of light." Then in eulogizing him, his son asked a rather pertinent question as to whether present-day society could produce a man of such great character: "Do they still make his kind?" he asked. It's an important question. Because everything we can see by the direction in which the world is going, begs for both light and direction.

Even the creators of AI have expressed concerns of its potential overreach. All of this should give us a jaw-dropping understanding of the confusion and chaos that can be expected. The disinformation around vaccines, lies about elections, lies about the history of enslavement, even attempts to revise the early beginnings of the United States. It is only the beginning.

Ephesians 5:6–8 tells us:

> *"Let no man deceive you with vain words: for because of these things cometh the wrath of God upon the children of disobedience. Be not ye therefore partakers with them. For ye were sometimes darkness, but now are ye light in the Lord: walk as children of light."*

The Message Bible (Eph. 5:8–10) puts it this way:

> *"You groped your way through that murk once, but no longer. You're out in the open now. The bright light of Christ makes your way plain. So no more stumbling around. Get on with it! The good, the right, the true—these are the actions appropriate for daylight hours. Figure out what will please Christ, and then do it."*

Light is desperately needed because the world, as we know it, is in darkness. Surely it is the understatement of the year, but we have to be intentional about seeking and displaying our inner Christian light. Christ, in us, is the Light of the World. Here are two of the many questions that should always be in the forefront of our minds. 1) What is the specific purpose of Christ-followers? 2) What is our purpose in this rapidly changing world? One significant response is to be light bearers. And that has already begun to take on new and extreme challenges that should force us to re-examine and update everything we have been doing as outreach and evangelism. In His Sermon on the Mount, Jesus was first stating the challenges of the Christian walk, then defining us, or rather stating who we are expected to become as His followers, giving us His blessing, and then His marching orders. Lights. Camera. Action. Go spread the Word; engage people; engage communities. Light up the world … at least your little corner of it. But before we can shed or share light, we have to build up the light within us. How do we build up the light to be a real disciple of Christ? We have to nurture a constant relationship with Him.

> *Light signifies readiness and direction for a journey. It is the way through the wilderness.*

If you have electricity but you don't plug it in, there will be no light. A battery that's not fully charged—no light. If you have a lovely, scented candle, but no matches with which to light it—no light. And, of course, we know the parable of the ten virgins. Lamp with no oil—no light. We have to prepare ourselves—charge our batteries, light our own candles, build up our inner spirit—before we can reach out to others.

Here are three suggestions:

- Twenty minutes of silent meditation every day. Use it to reflect on God's goodness, the many fires He has brought you through; contemplate your purpose
- Go to the source: Jesus. He said: "Peace I leave with you; my peace I give to you" (John 14:27, ESV). Connect with Him through His Word in your Bible.

The psalmist says: *"Thy word is a lamp unto my feet, and a light unto my path (Ps. 119:105).*

- Pray for direction, security, and guidance from the Spirit. Psalm 27:1: *"The Lord is my light and my salvation; whom shall I fear?"*

Light signifies readiness and **direction** for a journey. It is the way through the wilderness. This journey and this path are to guide us out of disinformation and false ideologies. It also carries with it **responsibility**. It means understanding **purpose (Ps. 119:105)** as it applies to preparation for **acting** and **sharing**.

We have to be deliberate, strategic, and thoughtful about witnessing. One of my church sisters sends out, by text, morning messages of encouragement, inspiration, and Bible texts. I read and share them with several friends far and wide. Sometimes I would get to it early, sometimes it would be late in the day, when I would read and pass it on. Sometimes people respond, more often than not, they don't. Or they just send you one of those thumbs-up symbols. No problem. I just leave it alone and let the Holy Spirit do its work. One day, however, I got a note from a girlfriend, a fast-paced New Yorker, who usually responded with the thumbs-up symbol. I know she's a busy New Yorker, so I wasn't even sure she was reading them. Surprisingly, she was. "Thanks for the daily messages," her text read, "but could you please send them earlier? I send it out to a bunch of my friends here, and they're asking me to send them earlier." One never knows how far one little light could shine. From Sis. Gina to me to my friend, Jen, touching lives near and far. It speaks to the spiritual impact we can have on people. We are not all expected to throw up a tent and preach for a week in order to reach people. You do what you are called to do, what you are led to do, no matter how small and insignificant it appears to be, and let the Holy Spirit do the rest. It is the responsibility of every one of us who calls ourselves Christ-followers.

Light illuminates untruth, evil, deception, indecision. It banishes fear. It gives clarity, so it provides the strength, courage, and holy boldness we all need to challenge and navigate this rapidly changing world. How can we use the light within us to influence people and change things around us? How can we, through our words and our deeds, draw people to the light of Christ?

These are questions we must consistently ask ourselves and be honest with ourselves. Depend on the leading of the Holy Spirit. Go brave! Go bold! We are a peculiar people, called to be representatives of God in a sin-sick world. God is depending on us to represent Him by our lives, sharing the good news that is our testimony of God's goodness and His grace.

We are blessed with the extraordinary privilege of having received the light of Christ. Let's make it our business to share one little light every day in even a small way, in word and/or deed.

*** *** ***

Guidance Text:
"Let your light so shine before men, that they may see your good works, and glorify your Father which is in heaven" (Matt. 5:16).

CHAPTER 16

THE DIVINE CONNECTION

"What's Love Got to Do With It?" the song title asks. "Everything," is the biblical prescription. It leads to a very personal question. Do you really know God? Or do you just know about Him? Therein lies one of the traps in the wilderness. As a maturing Christian, it was a conundrum that confronted and challenged me after a harrowing experience with a colleague and friend ... another friend with questionable motives.

In her capacity as a senior executive for a major international organisation, she hired contractors for special projects. I had successfully completed consulting contracts with her before, and we enjoyed a pleasant working relationship that developed into a friendship of sorts. Unknown to me, she had been navigating some of her own internal political hurdles and thought that I could provide her with useful information ... in exchange for another contract. Horrified at the prospect—apart from the fact that I had no inside information—I was appalled at the bold, callous, and unprofessional act of blackmail. I said as much, as delicately as I could and, needless to say, our friendship soured. Yet Daphne showed up at my house to visit my sister who was visiting from the US and to whom our friendship had extended. My sister left the room to get her a refreshment, just as I walked into the room to see Daphne get up, walk toward a glass door which, streaklessly clean, appeared to have been open. *BOOM* ... her head crashed into the door. I ran to make sure that she was fine and to get some ice for her forehead. She suffered no injury, thank God. A few months later, I was relating the story to my mother-in-law, ending with "God punished her for being so mean to me." To my surprise and embarrassment, Mama Sebro responded with a bemused look: "Meryl," she said, "God does not operate like that. God is a God of love."

News Flash: God is a God of love. It was a rude awakening that I still had a lot of work to do. I was entangled with weeds in the wilderness. Did I really know God for myself? Or did I just know **about** Him? More worrying. How do I know what I was being told about God was really who He is? I needed a deeper, more personal relationship with this God, a God who was far different from the "fire and brimstone" God with whom I was acquainted as a child. I had to know this God for myself ... not what I had read or had been preached. I had to have a stronger Divine connection. That was the point at which I re-read the Bible from cover to cover. I again struggled with parts of the King James version. Then an elderly uncle and aunt gave me a copy of *God's Victorious Army Bible* (Spiritual Warfare Edition II by Morris Cerullo). Little by little, I became armed and ready for battle. Later I consulted The Clear Word Bible, and The Women of Destiny Bible (a gift from Teacher Merle). But it is on The Message Bible, with its paraphrasing into contemporary language, that I now depend on for clarification. I listened to many religious sermons and presentations, visited many churches, and developed friendships with persons on a similar spiritual path, many far ahead of me. It was then I discovered the seeming male conspiracy to bury the women in the Bible. I used the research skills I had acquired in too many years at school and began writing. I specifically sought out female pastors to get some insight into their own experiences and was shocked but saddened that many of my concerns were on point. With a holy boldness, I would politely question male pastors at the end of sermons. For example, at a Resurrection Day service at a church in upstate New York, I questioned the pastor as to the reason he had neglected to mention the important fact that there were women at the foot of the cross; that women were the first to discover the risen Christ, and that a woman had been the very first person to speak to Him.

"Oh, yes," he agreed, and diplomatically dismissed me. The next Sunday, however, he was careful to include the presence of women in his sermon. Indeed, this recognition of the seeming conspiracy to overlook the representation of women in the Bible has led to my writing the two books on gender and religion, exploring the way in which the Word of God has been either intentionally or unknowingly misinterpreted, manipulated, or misdirected to mute women for one thing and to support, willfully or not, the subjugation of women. (*Genderstanding Jesus: Women in His View* and *Genderstanding: Leadership: Power to the Pew*.) Yet equality at the foot of the cross is undeniable. What could be clearer than Paul's reminder to the Galatians? Galatians 3:26–28:

> **For ye are all the children of God by faith in Christ Jesus. For as many of you as have been baptized into Christ have put on Christ. There is neither Jew nor Greek, there is neither bond nor free, there is nether male nor female: for ye are all one in Christ Jesus.**

Paul failed to include "there is neither Black, Brown, White, Native American, Hispanic, Indian, or Asian." But the inclusiveness in this powerful sentiment applies to us all. God loves us all—with our inglorious and sinful histories—with an unfathomable and incomprehensible love. And God created us to love Him. What's love got to do with it? Everything. He has made us for a close relationship with Him, so that He could guide and direct us through the treacherous traps the enemy sets for us. The traps of racism, racial violence, gender discrimination, domestic violence, economic inequality, hatred, white supremacy, Christian nationalism. We can be so easily trapped, even though we know, biblically, spiritually, and theoretically, what we must and how we should move.

During the writing of this chapter, I fell into such a trap. Don't judge. It was in the time of COVID. I was always particularly careful about touching the handles of doors in public spaces. I didn't use gloves, but I would arm myself with napkins or paper towels to open doors. Should anyone approach a door at the same time, I would be sure to hold the door for them, hopefully minimizing the spread of the disease through them. It had become a routine gesture for me, regardless of colour, ethnicity, age, or even gender.

One day, during the onslaught of the Omicron variant, I was exiting my favourite antique store. Antique lovers are some of the friendliest people you could meet. They are a chatty lot, always eager to comment on what you found, what you're looking for, to discuss and display their own finds, to share the best method of cleaning the antique you bought, and to tip you on the best antique spot or the latest antique sales. Antique lovers are the best.

On one of my antique shopping sprees, a tall, fiftyish Caucasian woman was exiting after me. I was masked; she was not, a major political statement in the battle of public health and security against massive misinformation and disinformation. It is a battle in which so-called Christians have been skillfully deceived by the enemy, I might add. By way of providing context—not absolution—this unfortunate drama unfolded in southwest Florida, at the height of the anti-vaccine movement, white supremacy, and violence against Black and Brown people; the discourse on critical race theory; the banning of books that even vaguely documented the struggle of Blacks against racism; right-wing extremism; voting rights suppression, and the concern of the impending threat of authoritarianism in the face of waning democracy. Florida was ground zero, a hot bed for all this negativism. With that hovering background, I still turned to hold the door to allow Ms. Lady to exit. The woman looked up with a cold, witheringly disdainful stare ... and then averted her eyes. I received the message of hate she had telegraphed with her eyes, and in a flash, I released the door, without looking back to see what had happened. I had estimated that there would have been enough time for her to grab the door without her being struck, yet gloated internally that my message had delivered the intended blow. I was fighting hate with hate. I reveled in smug self-satisfaction for about an hour. Okay, maybe half an hour ... and then a wave of self-disappointment, shame, and self-torment broke through. I spoke to no one about it. Sleep played hide and seek with me that night as I replayed the scene over and over in my head, still angry about the hate that I had sensed but more disappointed with my response. Interestingly, this sorry event had taken place while I had been about three months into an internal soul-search and a commitment to acquire the mind of Christ and to spread His light. I had failed myself; I had disappointed Jesus Christ. I had fallen into the trap of the enemy.

Successfully navigating the wilderness requires guidance from the Holy Spirit. To be like Jesus takes patience, mercy, forgiveness, loving ... and round-the-clock self-surveillance.

Successfully navigating the wilderness requires guidance from the Holy Spirit. To be like Jesus takes patience, mercy, forgiveness, loving ...

and round-the-clock self-surveillance. The enemy is always lurking, seeking prey to corral and destroy. That day, I was easy game. I played right into his/her hands. It brought home to me the urgency of always being on guard. When we least expect it, or when we are at our weakest point, he/she strikes. The biblical King David knows it better than any of us. Had he been leading his troops in the war, he would not have been trapped on his rooftop in the voyeurism that led to rape (yes, that ugly R word, given the power relations involved), deceit, and ultimately murder. Which is why he penned ***Psalm 51:10–12:***

"Create in me a clean heart, O God; and renew a right spirit within me. Cast me not away from thy presence; and take not thy holy spirit from me. Restore unto me the joy of thy salvation; and uphold me with thy free spirit."

Such is that Divine connection that embraces us with the prevenient grace ... the grace that goes before us to cover us even before we sin. That reliance on God comes through a trust that only comes with the knowledge of Him. Thankfully, we have now moved from the scare and fear of the "fire and brimstone" God that was preached ages ago to the true God of love, who blesses us with unmerited favour. In an ever-increasing world of hostility, violence, and hate, we will be called upon to seek even deeper measures of self-searching and self-examination.

In one of the virtual afternoon workshops my church holds on various issues of interest, the speaker, Minister Kwame Vanderhorst referred to a question his then pastor, Marcellus Robinson, asked the congregation about the most important commandment. He told of the surprise of the Seventh-day Adventist congregation that it was not the fourth commandment that commands us to remember and keep holy the seventh day of the week, to set it aside for rest and worship. It is the first commandment of love ... for God and for our neighbours as we love ourselves. And as if to reinforce this commandment, at the end of His earthly mission, Jesus Christ left His disciples with ***"a new commandment I give unto you, That ye love one another; as I have loved you, that ye also love one another. By this shall all men know that ye are my disciples, if ye have love one to another"*** **(John 13:34–35)**. Ouch! It is indeed a tall order that can only be fulfilled if we have a relationship with Him and are filled with and guided by the Holy Spirit.

Indeed, it occurred to me on the night of my sleepless self-evaluation that the environment of hate and hostility in which I am now surrounded is not one in which to reciprocate with hate but to stand out with inexplicable love, patience, and mercy. Tough task! Often it is easier said than done, but it means planning a strategy beforehand. For example, my husband and I have discussed how we would react should we ever be called the N-word face-to-face. My first smug reply was that I would ask the person to spell it, pointing to the studied ignorance that usually, though not exclusively, accompanies such racial animus. Such a response is clearly unacceptable when a verbal "turn-the-cheek" response is required. Full disclosure. I'm still working on it and praying that the Holy Spirit will indeed take over should I ever find myself in such a situation.

Undoubtedly, the need to have such conversations is paramount as we prepare for the perilous times that Bible-believing Christ-followers know are on the horizon. Even more confusing is that much of the direction emerging from the evangelical Christian churches comes closer to insensitivity to social justice at the very best, and at the more alarming extreme, a disregard, disassociation, and denial of common Christian values. It is for this reason that many, like me, shy away from the term, "Christians," for the more specific and intentional term, "Christ-followers." The bottom line is that Christian love is the only unifying and peace-making armour for such a time as this. The challenge for peace-seeking communities is, as simplistic as it may sound, to encourage love in the midst of the overwhelming and ever-increasing seasons of hate. What's love gotta do with it? Everything!

*** *** ***

Guidance Text:
"Beloved, let us love one another: for love is of God; and every one that loveth is born of God, and knoweth God" (1 John 4:7).

CHAPTER 17

LOVE IN THE TIME OF HATE

The many heart-breaking images and stories emerging from the ongoing slaughter in Ukraine are so devastating, that, like many of you, I sometimes shut my eyes and ears. But did you see the little boy in the colourful coat walking alone and bawling, probably because he had witnessed his parents killed? Two million children have now been forced to flee Ukraine, as the war rages on.[27] Traumatized children are unable to cry. The shock has knocked the living cry out of them. It is so painful to imagine children being deprived even of the ability to cry.

But the video clip that brought me to tears is the story of the child who was asked by a reporter what she had packed when forced to leave: "My colouring pencils," she said. "I sharpened all of them with long points so they would last a long time." "Show them to me," said the reporter. "I can't," the child replied. "I gave them away to my new friends I met on the train." Even a child, in hasty escape from the violent death and devastation in home and country, could take the time to share love with another, the

---

27 "Two million refugee children flee war in Ukraine in search of safety across borders," UNICEF, published March 30, 2022, https://1ref.us/wtw08.

actions of a child pointing to **the way** in which we should live—and **the way** we should love in this time of hate.

Acknowledgement that we are living in a time of war and incredible hate may be difficult for some, but this may not be new for many of us. Black and Brown people are among those considered to be on the margins of social, economic, and political society, and hence exposed to every imaginable level of hate. Hate for us is not new. But there is a new, renewed, organised, and structured hate that now exists. It is cold, bold, bare-faced, official hate, sanctioned by high office holders. Validated and normalized, hate has been legislated and written into the laws of many lands. Sadly, I live in one of the American states that is considered one of the hotbeds of this hate. Seemingly everything is being done to tighten the weave of this hate into the fabric of society. Mass shootings are on the rise. Religious leaders, precisely because of their visibility and power, have the power to spread peace, but many have opted for more confusion and chaos. This particular dynamic would be problematic for any new believer because of the mixed messages being sent, particularly around the politics of the election and re-election campaign of the forty-fifth president of the United States. Surely the discourse of hate did not begin there. But the level of hate that had been unleashed by the election and re-election of President Barack Obama as the forty-fourth president of the United States revealed an underbelly of rotten fruits, the stink spilling into every crevice of human interaction and institutions, including many religious organisations.

Perhaps the shooting at the Mother Emanuel African Methodist Episcopal (AME) Church in Charleston, South Carolina, is the textbook example of love in a time of hate. It is important to point out the historical significance of this church. When that young white man walked into a Wednesday night Bible study on June 17, 2015, he had to have known that it was the oldest Black church in the southern United States, founded in 1816. His research must have revealed that it was the first independent Black denomination in the United States, with roots to both enslaved Africans and free African Americans. Current attempts to bury Black history have a long and sordid past, but that young white supremacist may not have heard of Denmark Vesey, formerly enslaved, who had purchased his freedom and joined the AME Church in 1817, a year after it had been founded. A committed Christian, Vesey was a "class leader," and held home church during the week. Still, he was responsible for planning the most extensive rebellion in the history of the United States. Some scholars claim as many as 9,000 Blacks had been involved. The plan was discovered on the eve of the planned rebellion, and Vesey was eventually tried and hanged. Interestingly, four white men were fined and imprisoned for participating in the planned rebellion.[28]

But on the evening of that shooting, after the young white supremacist had been welcomed by the Bible study group, out of undiluted evil, hate, and anti-Black racism, he shot and killed nine persons, including the senior pastor, State Senator Clementa C. Pinkney, and injured one. Still, the response of the church members who survived the shooting was one of forgiveness and love. In the victims' statements at the court hearing, through her tears, the daughter of one of the victims said: "You took something very precious from me, but I forgive you.… It hurts me. You hurt a lot of people, but may God forgive you."[29] The granddaughter of Pastor Pinkney who was also killed said: "Although my grandfather and the other victims died at the hands of hate, this is proof that they lived and loved.… Hate won't win."[30] In their first public statement after the shooting, the family of the shooter said: "We have all been touched by the moving words from the victims' families offering God's forgiveness and love in the face of such horrible suffering."[31]

It remains clear that Christian love is the only unifying and peace-making force for such a time as this. The challenge for peace-seeking communities is, as simplistic as it may sound, to encourage love in the midst of the overwhelming and oncoming seasons of hate. I think repeatedly of that child on a train with refugees, giving away the colouring pencils she had so carefully sharpened and packed to occupy herself to children she met on the train, whom she thought needed them more than she did. The statements of the relatives of the victims of the Mother Emanuel AME Church come from a place of love that is incredibly rare. Yet, it is the law of a sovereign, forgiving God. That is truly an act of love in the time of hate.

> *It remains clear that Christian love is the only unifying and peace-making force for such a time as this.*

---

28   Kat Chow, "Denmark Vesey And The History Of Charleston's 'Mother Emanuel' Church," NPR, published June 18, 2015, https://1ref.us/wtw09.
29   Oliver Laughland, Paul Lewis, and Raya Jalabi, "'I forgive you': Charleston church victims' families confront suspect," The Guardian, June 19, 2015, https://1ref.us/wtw10.
30   Ibid.
31   Ibid.

Indeed, let us always be intentional about celebrating God's love, mercy, and grace and His unmerited favour, which He so generously showers on us.

*** *** ***

Guidance Text:
"But I say unto you, Love your enemies, bless them that curse you, do good to them that hate you, and pray for them which despitefully use you, and persecute you; that ye may be the children of your Father which is in heaven: for he maketh his sun to rise on the evil and on the good, and sendeth rain on the just and on the unjust" (Matt. 5:44–45).

CHAPTER 18

THE WAY

At its inception, this book was given many subtitles: *The Long and Winding Road* was one of the working titles, but it later became clear that the task set out was to document a long and winding road that indeed led through and out of the wilderness. The wilderness is wild. Beautiful. Dangerously beautiful. Untamed and loaded with traps and distractions. It is the setup for stumbles and missteps. "The *way*" is the passport out of doubt, uncertainty, confusion, and chaos. In other words, it is the path to meaningful and successful living. It became my personal challenge as a baby Christian. Many years later, as I matured—as previously mentioned—I would lament the new weaponizing of the word "Christian" to become a major political brand, hence my self-description as a Christ-follower.

The use of the word, "*way*," in the title of this chapter and the entire book became deliberate. It is the word the early Christ-followers used to refer to themselves. On the last night before His betrayal, Jesus encouraged His followers with one of His most powerful and instructive self-descriptions: "I am the *way*, the truth, and the life" (John 14:6). While the accepted interpretation of the word "*way*" is indeed the path chosen to follow Jesus

Christ, it might be a more instructive pun to link its meaning to the *way* in which Christians represent Christ.

"Ye shall know them by their fruits" (Matt. 7:16) is perhaps one of Jesus' most powerful nuggets of guidance for those of us who call ourselves by His name. On the other hand, it is a prophetic warning, now particularly timely as we are forced to sift through truth from error; to query the stances of so-called Christians who present a theology in direct contrast, even defiance, to the Word of God; and to determine how we treat others, especially those most different from who we are or what we believe. This is true for all of us, as we should all be intentional about producing good, healthy fruits. But "spoiled fruits" from those power brokers and influencers are even more glaring and destructive, precisely because of their visibility and power. It is an old, old story.

While I did not fully consider myself a mature Christian, but a Christian under construction, I was anchored enough to the Word of God to be horrified by the blatant and strategic misrepresentation of the Word. It forced me to be more purposed and intentional about seeking cover under His wings. I came to understand that it is only in the context of a true understanding of the age-old cosmic struggle between good and evil that one understands the inevitability of the conflict.

Breaking news: God is a God of love. Of course, we all know that. But let it sink in for a moment. God is a God of love.

1 John 4:7–8:

Beloved, let us love one another: for love is of God; and every one that loveth is born of God, and knoweth God. He that loveth not knoweth not God; for God is love.

We may know it, internalize it, and show it … most of the time. But how are we as Christ-followers to react when the hate hits us smack in the face?

We know that the core of this hate is inequality. Inequality as a strategy to ensure power. Yet equality at the foot of the cross is undeniable. What could be clearer than Paul's reminder to the Galatians in **Galatians 3:26–28:**

For ye are all the children of God by faith in Christ Jesus. For as many of you as have been baptized into Christ have put on Christ. There is neither Jew nor Greek, there is neither bond nor free, there is neither male nor female: for ye are all one in Christ Jesus.

Paul failed to include "there is neither Black, Brown, White, African or Caribbean, Native American, or Hispanic or Indian or Asian, young or old." But the inclusiveness in this powerful sentiment applies to us all. God loves us all—with all of our inglorious and sinful missteps and histories—with an unfathomable and incomprehensible love. And God created us to love Him. He has made us for a close relationship with Him, so that He could guide and direct us through the treacherous traps the enemy sets for us in the wilderness. Traps that will tempt, even force, us to respond contrary to His divine direction. The traps of racism, racial violence, gender discrimination, domestic violence, economic inequality, hatred, white supremacy. We can be so easily trapped, even though we know biblically, spiritually, and theoretically what we must be about … how we should move. How we should represent Jesus. How we should love. The temptation is particularly true in this time when seemingly there is permission to behave badly. I'm talking about love in a time of hate.

My mind returns repeatedly to that Ukrainian child on a train of refugees, giving the coloured pencils she had so carefully sharpened and packed to occupy herself; yet she gave away the pencils to children she met on the train whom she thought needed them more than she did. That is truly love in the time of hate. I have to confess, for all the sadness I felt, and the prayers I sent up for the Ukrainians, I was again challenged when I saw Ukrainian officials pushing African female students off the train and telling them to "walk." Or sending the Africans to the back of the line as they tried to board the train. One woman from Nigeria had to walk twelve hours to get to the bus that would take her to the Ukrainian border. When she arrived there, tired, cold, and hungry … she said she had been walking in her sleep. The official told her: "You Black. You walk." Tired and hungry, she walked another eight hours, where she was pushed and beaten before she could cross the border into Poland.

Racism is real, and it is painful. I live in Florida, one of its hot spots. And, yes, we are still expected to love, in a time of intense hate.

> *We love him, because he first loved us. If a man say, I love God, and hateth his brother, he is a liar: for he that loveth not his brother whom he hath seen, how can he love God whom he hath not seen? And this commandment have we from him, That he who loveth God love his brother also.*
>
> **(1 John 4:19–21)**

The need to put self aside and to pray for the full unction of the Holy Spirit to break barriers, and to show love, mercy, and forgiveness could not be more urgent. Interestingly, some of the most instructive words on that fateful night of the slap heard and felt around the world, came from the actor, Denzel Washington, to fellow-actor, Will Smith: "Be careful. At your highest moment, that's when the devil comes for you."

A lay pastor at church not long ago referred to Satan as an "unemployed cherubim" who was redoubling his efforts because he knows his time is short. "Don't hate," he urged us. "Celebrate so you can participate." Indeed, for all of its current and increasing challenges, it is critical to be intentional about celebrating God's love, mercy, and grace: His unmerited favour.

> *But God, who is rich in mercy, for his great love*
> *wherewith he loved us.*
> *Even when we were dead in sins, hath quickened us*
> *Together with Christ, (by grace ye are saved).*
>
> *(Eph. 2:4–5)*

Let us keep close to our hearts this love note to you and to me from *1 John 4:7–8*:

> *Beloved, let us love one another: for love is of God; and everyone that loveth is born of God, and knoweth God. He that loveth not knoweth not God; for God is love.*

The stark absence of basic humanity and Christ-like love appears to characterize current world *zeitgeist*. The wilderness is chock-full of land mines at every twist and turn, with GPS systems often inoperative or deliberately giving incorrect and/or confusing directions. My own journey clearly points to the need for foolproof guidance. It can only be found in the Word of God. In His ultimate wisdom, God has revealed the whole journey: the beginning, the accidents, diversions, the stop lights, potholes; then He sent a conductor, Jesus Christ, His Son, who did His leg of the journey and passed the baton to our spiritual guide, the Holy Spirit. What a magnificent God we serve! The problem, however, is that we are so intimidated by the raw power of our spiritual Guide that we ignore Him to our own peril.

Spiritual guidance is particularly critical in the extraordinarily perilous times in which we now live, regardless of place, space, privilege, age, ethnicity, or religious belief. We all need to carefully monitor and draw strength from our own lived experiences and those of others. I think of the Brooklyn woman who, uncharacteristically, fell asleep on the subway the morning of the 9/11 tragedy. She had slept past her stop, and in trying to get back, missed the explosion of the Twin Towers where she worked. In a similar experience, on that fateful day, another woman broke her shoe heel and returned home to change shoes. That broken shoe heel was the hidden blessing that enabled her to escape the tragedy at her place of work where many of her co-workers were killed. In a more recent tragedy at this writing, a man in Buffalo, New York, left his home on the way to the supermarket to quickly pick up some groceries for Saturday evening dinner. In a quick change of mind, he decided to buy dinner instead of groceries and turned right to a restaurant instead of left to the grocery. That left turn would have led him to the TOPS grocery, where he could have become the eleventh person shot by the young, deranged racist.

In a less-deadly event, I draw from my own lived experience during a pre-Thanksgiving family dinner. A freak accident resulted in the crashing of a glass table in my breakfast nook. It began a long and time-consuming search for a wooden table that was sturdy but small enough to fit into the breakfast nook. After the first month of searching, I decided to pray about it and was clearly directed to a particular store. I visited the store about four times. The tables were lovely but were the wrong shape (I was looking for oblong); most of them were round or the dreaded glass instead of wood. Six months later, I still hadn't found the table.

In the height of frustration, I went to another store and found a table that appeared to be suitable. I was not excited about it, but frustration outmatched good sense, and obedience to the Spirit, I hasten to add. It was not the store to which the Spirit had directed me and to which I had gone several times, with fruitless results. The morning of the delivery, the nice lady at the store called to inform me that the movers had discovered a crack in one of the legs of the table. It had been repaired and sealed, but the sealing was still visible. She was willing to return my money—against store policy—or if I still wanted the table, she would return 50 percent of the cost, thereby selling it to me at half the price.

That crack in the table leg was clearly a red flag, one that I overruled, dazzled by the prospect of paying half the price and the impatience of getting a replacement table. I agreed to take the table. When the table arrived, and the two young men settled it into the spot which I had meticulously cleared, it was apparent that the table was too high. I could live with that,

I argued against my better judgment. Then the men called me to point out that they felt the repaired leg looked a bit tentative. Even though the leg was still sturdy, the crack had widened. All it would take was a little wood glue, the kind man said. Wood glue? This was getting a bit out of control. Quickly I got the nice lady on the phone and humbly admitted that I had made the wrong decision. We agreed that I could return the table but only receive half of the delivery fee for the return.

Why is this story instructive? First, it is a classic example of the interjection of the **Spirit** in our daily lived experiences. Women are particularly in tune with the working of the Holy Spirit in our lives, and many women's devotionals detail pore-raising stories of divine intervention and deliverance in the jaws of defeat. Secondly, there is the **trust** factor. Central to a Spirit-led life is trusting in divine guidance. I was specifically directed to the store at which I would find the table, but my trust and patience were overcome by the frustrations of not finding the table after several visits.

> *Trust in the Lord with all your heart,*
> *and do not lean on your own understanding.*
> *In all your ways acknowledge him,*
> *and he will make straight your paths.*
>
> *Proverbs 3:5 (ESV)*

And then there is **obedience.** How much easier it is to obey when in our limited minds it makes good sense. But it is when we are Spirit-guided to do what seems to be untenable for us that we are called to obey. It is the Abraham-like obedience, taking his only son—for whom he had waited such a long time—to be sacrificed. That is the big challenge. It is where the trust factor reigns. "Trust and obey, for there's no other way,"[32] says the song.

Just as we get the big two—**trust and obedience**—nailed down, there's **patience.** Undoubtedly it is my own Achilles heel, as the table story clearly reveals. How difficult it is for us to wait ... patiently, in the middle of our personal storms. Yet, the Word clearly says:

> *"But they that wait upon the Lord shall renew their strength; they shall mount up with wings as eagles; they shall run, and not be weary; and they shall walk, and not faint." (Isa. 40:31)*

---

32 J.H. Sammis and Daniel B. Towner, *The Seventh-day Adventist Hymnal*, "Trust and Obey" (Hagerstown, MD: Review and Herald Publishing Association, 1985), p. 590.

It is that eagle strength, promised by patiently waiting, that we need to navigate these perilous times. Sure-footed, steadfast, single-minded, solid in His Word, and guided by His Spirit: these are my own goals and my wish for every reader. I have been blessed to be able to read and spell, I like to say, and so far, I have not come across a more proven route out of the wilderness to the way that leads to a glorious heaven. I hope and pray to be there. I pray and hope to see you there.

Let the choir sing: HALLELUJAH!

TOPS:

- **Trust Him**
- **Obey Him**
- **Patience**
- **Spirit Led**

As Jesus Himself ended His Sermon on the Mount as documented in **Matthew 5:48:**

"Be ye therefore perfect, even as your
Father which is in heaven is perfect."

*** *** ***

Guidance Text:
"But I say unto you, Love your enemies, bless them that curse you, do good to them that hate you, and pray for them which despitefully use you, and persecute you" (Matt. 5:44).

CHAPTER 19

ANSWERING THE CALL

The phone call was sudden and unwelcome. The solemn voice at the other end of the phone introduced himself as a representative of Life Alert, a service for the advanced in age who live alone, usually by choice. His words were cold with authority. "Are you Meryl James-Sebro?" My identity being established, the voice wasted neither time nor emotion. "Do you know Beverly James?" "Yes, she is my sister," my voice icy with fear. "She fell in her home, and we have taken her to the ER." With a frozen heart I thought of her only son, Alaistair, who lived in another state and would be next alerted. I lived a solid three and a half hours away by road, but I would get there before him. Thus began the nineteen-day journey that took my sister—my only sibling—to the ER and me to an unimaginable spiritual confrontation. Beverly's struggle with asthma from childhood was a storied one. This saga would unfurl slowly with sharp curves, ups and downs, round-the-clock prayers from many states and countries and whooping hallelujahs. What I didn't realise then, was the battleground I was about to enter, and the test of my own spiritual maturity.

The warfare began as early as 5:30 the next morning as my husband, Tony, and I headed out on the three and a half hour road trip to the hospital to which my sister had been taken. One hour into the trip, however, an accident-related traffic jam held us in a vicious vise for more than two hours that turned the trip into an almost six-hour, bladder-tormented one. Had we paid proper attention, we would have noted the beginning of the spiritual warfare that persisted and would have been better prepared.

We finally arrived to find her physically weakened, with a bruised forehead but defiant and in total command of her situation ... or so she thought. "The doctors have a plan, but I have my own plan," she assured Tony. A hyper-efficient intensive care (ICU) and operating room (OR) nurse for more than half of the fifty-four years she worked in New York's challenging health care system, she was no stranger to the mistakes that could be made in administering health care. Hence, in spite of her own compromised health condition, she was in full professional mode, advocating for herself as persistently as she had for the thousands of patients she had tended. About two weeks before tripping and falling at her front door, she had been equipped with an oxygen supply system to facilitate her increasing breathing issues. The panic of the fall and the ambulance trip to the hospital may well have produced an asthma attack. Whatever the reason, the attending physicians were determined not to release her to her home, where she lived alone. The focus then became one of finding a reliable and comfortable facility in which she could get the required medical care and personal security. Our research led us to a spanking-new facility close to the hospital. Tony and I returned home as Alaistair, her only child, flew in to monitor her continuing hospitalized care and complete arrangements for the transfer. We continued to be prayerful and hopeful.

Arrangements having been made, and the transfer completed, we were confident all was going well, with the full understanding that her total recovery would be slow. Three phone calls from her son followed: the first, that she had settled into this friendly, modern facility and into a room with a lovely view. The second call brought further encouraging news, that having settled in nicely, she was to be taken to be evaluated: the routine checking of vital signs, overall status, etc. The next phone call, however, turned the page: dehydrated and with vital signs of some concern, she would have to be returned to the hospital. There, the same hospital that had discharged her to the facility, directed her from the emergency room to the intensive care unit (ICU).

Tony and I had hardly settled back home when we were back on the road, thankfully spared of accident-related traffic jams. By the time we arrived, Beverly was somewhat stabilized but so unresponsive to treatment that hospice care was being considered. However, she was having none of it. Guided by her written living will instructions, we prayerfully rejected it. My sister seemed to have received a spurt of energy from her granddaughter and daughter-in-law who had flown in from New York, and was returned to a normal room. But that, too, was short-lived. The next day she was taken back to the ICU. We had returned home to keep a doctor's appointment but returned to the hospital a day or two later to find her in a situation of increased concern on many levels. In addition, or probably because of the prayerful support received from our own church, the Golden Gate All Nations Seventh Day Adventist Church in Naples, Florida, and prayer groups and prayer warriors in Trinidad, the UK, Canada, Nigeria, Jamaica, etc., the enemy was on the warpath.

At one point, Tony and Alaistair left the room for a quick break and man-to-man chat when the hospital erupted in a cacophony of alarm bells and buzzers, accompanied by blazing lights. Doctors, nurses, and techs were buzzing around like bees in a hive. Suddenly all the corridors were empty of computers and equipment set up outside the rooms. Full lockdown. I tried to ask whether this was a real emergency or a mere fire drill. The bees returned blank stares, signaled me back into her room, and slammed shut the heavy door. I thought of opening it to peep outside, but it dawned on me that in the violent space in which we all now find ourselves, there could be a shooter. Instead, I texted my husband. "Is there a fire? Or a fire drill?" No response. I peeped through the tightly closed window, saw the red lights of an ambulance, and assumed the worst, forgetting that the room was several floors above the emergency room. Of course, that could easily explain an ambulance with flashing lights ... to a rational mind. I moved closer to my sister's bedside, prayed silently, and thought out a plan to smash the window to lift her out and rescue us both, should I even get a whiff of smoke. I confess to an overactive imagination, so I immediately began to smell smoke. But then, thankfully, the alarms stopped as suddenly as they had started, and smiling bees, calmly, but still without explanation, returned to open the door and replace the stations in the corridors. That night, as I relived the situation, I felt that my panic did not favourably represent my Christian walk. Did I pray enough? Did I trust enough in God's protective covering? More importantly, was I praying enough for my sister's health condition? Suddenly the scales of denial dropped from my eyes. Those alarm bells were for me. Beverly had neither eaten nor spoken for two days. I needed to be more concerned about my sister's soul, not her body.

The next day, a sunny Sunday morning, I waited until my husband and nephew were out of the room, and I went into action. Beve appeared to be sleeping, but in sharing her nursing experience with us, she had always explained that hearing was the last to go. Armed with that information, I held her hand, bent over her, and cried out to the Lord. I thanked God for her life; I reminded Him of who He was and whose she was. I pleaded the blood of Jesus; I broke every chain and bound every demon in His mighty name. I promised that her life and struggle over nicotine would be a testimonial, still thinking she would be the one giving it. I prayed for the forgiveness of sins and the presence of the Holy Spirit. I prayed until my mouth was dry and my tongue stuck to the roof of my mouth. I had no more words. I took a quick breath and started to sing. For the life of me, I couldn't remember any of the victory songs we sang lustily in church. A few days before, in coaxing Beve to use the oxygen mask, I had sung our grandmother's favourite hymn "Higher Ground," with the refrain:

> *Lord, lift me up and I shall stand, by faith on heaven's table land. A higher plane than I have found; Lord, plant my feet on higher ground.*[33]

Even before I sang the last line of the hymn, I could see her pushing her legs up in the bed, in anticipation of the line that she remembered, "Lord plant my feet on higher ground." But not even that song came to my mind. All I could sing was the "A-men A-men A-A-men Amen Amen," made popular by the 1963 Sidney Poitier movie, "Lilies of the Fields." At the same time that my tired voice began to wane, my sister suddenly joined me with her own "A-men A-men," and then, with surprising strength, "Hallelujah, Hallelujah, Hallelujah! "Yes, Beverly," I said. "That's the highest praise." And we both continued to give Him the praise He deserves. Hallelujah! Thankfully, I was able to retrieve my phone from wherever it usually hides itself to record part of that praise session, not only to comfort my nephew and my husband but to assure myself that what I thought I heard was not exhaustion and an overworked imagination. I shared the audio clip with them that night. Soon after, we were summoned to the hospital for my nephew to give permission to increase her oxygen level. As sleep began to overcome her, I whispered in her ear: "Sleep sweetly, sis. When you wake up, you will see the bright, shining face of Jesus." I meant it would be a beautiful, sunny day, one in which she would be feeling much better. But I seemed to have been speaking prophetically. Beverly made her peaceful

---

33 Johnson Oatman, Jr. and Charles H. Gabriel, *The Seventh-day Adventist Hymnal*, "Higher Ground" (Hagerstown, MD: Review and Herald Publishing Association, 1985), p. 625.

transition early the next morning. Later I would be reminded of the text: ***"And call upon me in the day of trouble: I will deliver thee, and thou shalt glorify me" (Ps. 50:15).***

At this writing, it is less than three months since my sister's passing but enough time to begin to be thankful for the magnificent gift that God has given to our family in knowing that my sister had glorified Him with her last breath. Surely, she will be among the "dead in Christ shall rise first" (1 Thess. 4:16). For the first time, I think I truly understand the promise that all Christ-followers know so well: "The peace … which passeth all understanding" (Phil. 4:7).

In the Caribbean, it is often said that "God *doh* make a mistake." The Barbadians, in particular, claim that God wears pyjamas, but He never sleeps. These two sayings are worth remembering as we wait on God for an answer to our prayers. I had prayed for years for my sister, a seasoned medical professional, to kick the nicotine habit. After her death, we found evidence of the many attempts and strategies she had indeed tried. It was a forbidden topic of conversation and often the source of a degree of sourness. Our bodies are indeed our temples, and I was afraid a temple sullied with smoke wound be unacceptable to our heavenly Father. Clearly this is unadulterated arrogance on my path, since the Bible clearly states that our thoughts are not His (**Isa. 55:8**). When we pray, we are not entitled to direct God, the supreme Creator how, what, why, when, or whether He should accomplish our request. He is God all by Himself; He knows the beginning from the end, and He will do what's best for us—but in His time. My prayer was indeed answered and without my mortal help. For the nineteen days that my sister had been hospitalized, she was unable to smoke. There were so many twists and turns that, in retrospect, pointed to how our patient Father was preparing Beve for her transition. My single prayer had been reinforced by the prayers of the saints wherever in the world they were. This experience was indeed a master class in **intercessory prayer**. Prayer that soars overseas, hurdles oceans, ignores space, and defies distance to reach the throne room. Hallelujah!

One of the biggest traps, however, is unforgiveness. My sister had been estranged from one of our cousins, a second cousin who had been responsible for her retirement in Florida. In fact, she had been her chief advisor and *de facto* supervisor in the building of her retirement home while my sister still lived in New York. But they had fallen out over a well-needed discussion on her smoking, the discussions that I had deliberately avoided, and our cousin had dared. I struggled with whether I should call our cousin, who lived a mere ten minutes away. I prayed about it, and my husband insisted that I call her. I hesitated, prayed about it again, then my husband threatened to call her himself. That forced me to make the telephone call. Our cousin visited twice: once when Beve was still coherent and there had been an amicable reunion. On her second visit, however, my sister had already minimized or ceased communication. Still, the many twists and turns had enabled the reconciliation and the peace with which she eventually passed.

Much has been written about the danger of the absence of forgiveness and its risk of blocking God's grace. When we think of God's grace, His unmitigated favour in forgiving our sins, how dare we not forgive others? Moreover, how dare we not forgive ourselves, often the root of social friction and self-imposed stress?

Forgiveness is the calling card of God's amazing love. It seems to have been one of the keys to the release my sister needed for her peaceful transition. God's love, faithfulness, and patience in seeking and waiting on us are reflections of the gift of the salvation received through the death and resurrection of His Son, Jesus Christ. Indeed, His goodness is running after us, as the popular gospel song goes. If only we could stand long enough to be completely embraced and consumed by it. His mercy and goodness follow us once we commit to Him and leave ourselves open to His redeeming grace. Hallelujah!

It is even more amazing that God is depending on us, not only to accept His **goodness**, but to spread it. Paul tells us that he is convinced that we are **"full of goodness, filled with knowledge and competent to instruct one another"** *(Rom. 15:14, NIV)*. What a challenge! What a responsibility! The theologians refer to it as the "priesthood of all believers." It is the belief that instead of a priestly class of humans, all believers become priests through their union with Christ. We believers *"are a chosen generation, a royal priesthood, an holy nation, a peculiar people; that ye should shew forth the praises of him who hath called you out of darkness into his marvellous light" (1 Peter 2:9)*. It is a role that is often forced on us, as it was in my final experience with my sister. In responding to my sister's need, however, I was forced to find, claim, and operationalise my **power**, my **authority**, and my **responsibility** as a believer, as a Christ-follower. We are blessed to have been chosen to represent Him at one of the most turbulent times in human history. Our challenge is to understand and equip ourselves for the purpose for which we have been called. We must prepare ourselves to accept and execute the responsibility placed upon us at a moment's notice. I almost missed a critical moment by focusing on our physical safety during the lockdown at the hospital. Thankfully, I was given another chance to re-examine my place, position, and my purpose. These end-time days indeed call for readiness for the work we all have to do.

Following the *way* leaves footprints on that narrow path through the wilderness so others might follow. It lights the way so that others might see and follow His light in and to His way. May we all listen for the call and answer appropriately when it comes. Amen.

Guidance Text:
"Restore us, O God; cause Your face to shine, and we shall be saved" **(Ps. 80:3, NKJV).**

The author (r) and sister, Beverly James (1944–2023)

CHAPTER 20
FULL CIRCLE

In the preceding chapters, my stories are meant to reveal a focus on our relationship with the Divine Trinity, not religion. I pray they have accomplished that. Here are some thought-provoking questions for honest, serious self-talk.

- Is your relationship with God just a head knowledge? Is it a transactional, "gimme, gimme" one? Or is it a heart-understanding that leads to action?
- Are you comfortable and complacent about the "covering" of religion? Or are you daily seeking the infilling of the Holy Spirit to do the work for which you have been called and only you can do?

This is an unending conversation, all of which we already know but all of which we need to be intentional about practicing. We are familiar with the drill: Pray. Pray. Pray. If you have not yet had one of those amazingly scary and awesome moments when God dramatically answers a prayer, then pray some more. Challenge God. Try Him with situations you think unfixable. He is your Father; your Friend; your Protector; your Provider;

your Saviour. He loved us so much that He sent His Son to die for us. He knows our thoughts and concerns. He will certainly answer your prayer, one way or another. Just be patient and trust Him. Oh, for an opportunity to respond like Job:

> *"I have heard of thee by the hearing of the ear; but now mine eye seeth thee" (Job 42:5).*

The Message Bible breaks it down:

> *"I admit I once lived by rumors of you;*
> *now I have it all firsthand—from my own eyes and ears!"*

Let me repeat, for emphasis, two key relationship tips:
Stay in the Word:

Extra spiritual ammunition is required for this end-time spiritual battle. We need to be prepared. The psalmist says:

> *"O taste and see that the LORD is good: blessed is the man [or woman] that trusteth in him" (Ps. 34:8).*

The Message Bible is more direct and dramatic:

> *"Open your mouth and taste, open your eyes and see—*
> *how good God is.*
> *Blessed are you who run to him."*

Get to Know His Voice:

Years ago, I overheard my mother-in-law witnessing to a friend and telling her about her conversations with God. "How do you know it's God talking to you?" the woman asked. Without missing a beat, Mama Sebro replied: "Satan doesn't talk to me anymore. Any voice I hear I know is the voice of God!"[34] *Boom*! When you have spent time with God, you get to know His voice, to **trust** Him; to **follow** His lead; to **know** His purpose for your life; and to **move** in complete sync with His **guidance**. Hallelujah! That is relationship-building.

So let me conclude with a few questions that we should all think about.

---

34 Editor's note: This anecdote is intended to highlight the importance of a deep relationship with God, but not to imply human infallibility or immunity from Satan's temptations.

The first is that age old question: Do we know God? Or do we just know about Him? In 1 Corinthians 4:20, Paul writes to the Corinthians, "For the kingdom of God is not in word, but in power." He is saying that God's kingdom is not just about talk or big ideas. The Message Bible calls it "***hot air***," and continues: ***"God's Way is not a matter of mere talk; it's an empowered life."*** It is about action. Service. Power. But this power of God is available only through faith in Christ and the Holy Spirit.

Courage and Purpose. The fact that we are here in this time, season, and place means that each of us has work to do ... a special purpose to fulfill. So, GO **BRAVE**! Bind the spirit of fear. "God hath not given us the spirit of fear; but of power, and of love, and of a sound mind" (2 Tim. 1:7).

As related, my spiritual journey began attending the Seventh-day Adventist church with my grandmother and continued in the Roman Catholic Church. As an adult, however, my spiritual adventure received the most stabilizing grounding from the Agape Ministries Full-Gospel Church in Trinidad, under the headship of Pastor Samuel Philip, and later from the Celebration Church in Columbia, Maryland, under the headship of Pastor Robert Davis, Sr. and later, his son, Pastor Robbie Davis, Jr.

My husband, the son of a Seventh-day Adventist pastor, is grounded in the Seventh-day Adventist faith, supported by an expansive network of wonderful faith-filled family, friends, and associates from his SDA Christian education. Avoiding the weeds of the different days of worship but intent on remaining firm in my faith, I attended church on both Saturday and Sunday. Theologically, the major difference is the SDA's focus on rest and worship on the seventh day, and the state of the dead. According to SDA doctrine, once "transitioned," we remain asleep until the second coming of Jesus Christ **(1 Thess. 4:16–17)**:

> *For the Lord himself shall descend from heaven with a shout, with the voice of the archangel, and with the trump of God: and the dead in Christ shall rise first: Then we which are alive and remain shall be caught up together with them in the clouds, to meet the Lord in the air: and so shall we ever be with the Lord.*

Setting aside the entire day on Saturday for rest, worship, and quality time with the Creator not only made good sense; it also supplied the peace, calm, and respite that bolstered me through many personal, academic, and professional life challenges. Moreover, it afforded a profound study and understanding of the Word that supported a distinction between the God of love, with whom I had developed a relationship and the "fire and brimstone" God to whom I was introduced as a child.

The author and husband, Anthony Sebro Sr.

And then on Sunday morning, much later than the women who had trekked to His empty tomb on that glorious Sunday morning of His resurrection, I would join the praise and worship in song and dance that truly exposed my soul to His glory and the victorious power of His resurrection. However, the physical and logistical challenges of going to church on both Saturday and Sunday eventually overwhelmed me. I took the path of least resistance and began going to church only on Saturdays, then became truly physically and spiritually refreshed and blessed by this practice of honouring and keeping the Sabbath on the true Lord's Day.

> ***If thou turn away thy foot from the sabbath, from doing thy pleasure on my holy day; and call the sabbath a delight, the holy of the Lord, honourable; and shalt honour him, not doing thine own ways, nor finding thine own pleasure, nor speaking thine own***

words: Then shalt thou delight thyself in the Lord; and I will cause thee to ride upon the high places of the earth, and feed thee with the heritage of Jacob thy father: for the mouth of the Lord hath spoken it. (Isa. 58:13–14)

Later, encouraged by my brother-in-law, Dr. Walter Douglas, a retired SDA pastor and chairman *emeritus* of the theology department at Andrews University, one of my spiritual advisors, I would become a Seventh-day Adventist by profession of faith. That move allowed me to serve as director of women's ministries at the Golden Gate All Nations Seventh-day Adventist Church in Naples, Florida, for six years and later as its head of communications.

Those "in-between" years, however, afforded me careful study of the Word, discussions with theologians, and fellowship with serious believers. Specially heaven-sent gifts came in the package of reconnection with a Nigerian sister-friend who, in her own spiritual journey, had become Pastor Lola Alakija, in addition to close friendships with US-based Pastor Brenda Billingy, pastor emerita of two SDA churches in Maryland, who became central in the struggle over women's ordination in the Seventh-day Adventist church, and Barbados-based Apostle Dr. Lucille Baird, founder and CEO of Mount Zion's Missions, whose bold and uncompromising broadcasting of the Word continues to speak truth to power and to challenge the Caribbean to a deeper spirituality. These relationships provided laser-focused opportunities to observe, to learn, to re-learn, and to question—if not to outright decipher—truth from error. I began to distinguish between Scripture and traditions that had long lost currency and applicability. Most critically, I depended solely on the Word of God as documented and represented in many of the contemporary translations I have made it my business to acquire.

Perhaps not surprisingly, the post-Obama period in the United States has unleashed a degree of hate, violence, xenophobia, antisemitism, and a white supremacy rebirth and remix that led to a particular interest in the book of Revelation and its dramatic end-time prophecies. In its wake, COVID-19 has left such a spate of near cataclysmic concerns about physical, environmental, political, social, moral, and spiritual health that even confirmed and unapologetic atheists and agnostics have begun to observe and openly discuss the end of earth's history. The political extreme right has so influenced US white evangelists that a Christian nationalism has emerged that is so dangerous in its diametric contradiction to biblical mandates that Christ Himself would have objected. Global, political, and religious systems were and are continuing to unite with record speed, aided by the input of technology that, for all its benefits, has proven to display undisputed, functional malevolence. "Through the two great errors, the immortality of the soul, and Sunday sacredness, Satan will bring the people under his deceptions."[35] This is where the rubber meets the road, and we, as Christ-followers, will be forced to make serious decisions about whom we worship.

For me, organised religion still presents many questions, doubts, and challenges, specifically with respect to race/ethnicity and gender. The fact that I am associated with a religious organisation that rejects the ordination of women remains a nagging, internal debate, and brings many frustrating moments when, I, unapologetically, make a nuisance of myself. Ongoing insensitivities to women in sermons and other ways underscore the need for continuing work. The takeaway, however, is the critical importance of, not religion, but relationship … a connection with the Divinity that cannot be dulled by human frailties. A Divine connection. Forgive the repetition, but we need to know God for ourselves, not just to merely know about Him. We need to document, enjoy, and share our experiences with Him. It is the only way we can know that God is really who He says He is … not what others tell us about Him.

The challenging and unprecedented times in which we are blessed to be living call for strength, courage, and purpose. The fact that you and I are here in this time, season, and place—wherever that might be—means that we have work to do. We are on assignment, with a specific purpose to fulfill. This intimate discernment and relationship with God supersede any connection to religion and transfer to us the power, peace, and purpose of His presence in our lives. This clarity of thought, intention, and action prioritizes a focus on the Divine that will stand the many tests and traps that stubbornly attempt to waylay or ambush true truth seekers. Our faith, our trust, and our hope in Jesus Christ and His soon coming remain our only ammunition. So, go brave! Bind the spirit of fear. "God hath not given us the spirit of fear; but of power, and of love, and of a sound mind" (2 Tim. 1:7). Amen!

Go brave. Shine His light. *Vaya con Dios!*
MARANATHA!!!

***   ***   ***

---

35   Ellen G. White, The Great Controversy 1888 (Mountain View, CA: Pacific Press, 1888), p. 588.

Guidance Text:
"Stand fast therefore in the liberty wherewith Christ hath made us free, and be not entangled again with the yoke of bondage" (Gal. 5:1).

Prayer: *God of our weary years ... God of our silent tears; God of our frantic fears; God who is always near ... ahead and behind. Protect our hearts and make them stronger and more supple to expand our ability to love in the midst of hate. So, Father, clothe us in Your glory; point us to your love, so we can love more when we are hated; be at peace in the midst of violence; be joyous in hope and, above all, to keep the faith through the beauty You have provided for us, and to be ready for the purpose for which You have prepared us. And please, Lord, come soon to take us home from the mess of this world. Amen and amen.*

BIBLIOGRAPHY

Burton, Keith. *The Blessing of Africa: The Bible and African Christianity.* Downers Grove, IL: InterVarsity Press, 2007.

Cone, James. *A Black Theology of Liberation.* Maryknoll, NY: Orbis Books, 1986.

Cone, James. *Said I Wasn't Gonna Tell Nobody.* Maryknoll, NY: Orbis Books, 2018.

Gates, Jr. Henry Louis. *The Black Church: This is Our Story, This is Our Song.* New York, NY: Penguin Press, 2021.

James-Sebro, Meryl. *Genderstanding Leadership: Power to Pew!* Bloomington, IN: WestBow Press, 2015.

James-Sebro, Meryl. *Genderstanding Jesus: Women in His View.* New York, NY: TEACH Services, Inc., 2005.

Mbiti, John S. *African Religions and Philosophies.* Garden City, NY: Anchor Books, 1969.

Tolbert, Emory, ed. *2000 Years of Christianity in Africa*. Washington, D.C.: Howard University Press, 2005.

Warren, Rick. *The Purpose Driven Life*. Grand Rapids, MI: Zondervan, 2002.

White, Ellen G. *The Great Controversy*. Altamont, TN: Harvestime Books, 1888.

Wilkerson, Isabel. *Caste: The Origins of Our Discontents*. New York, NY: Random House, 2020.

Yankson, Sednak, K. D. *Africa's Roots in God*. Hempstead, NY: Sankofa Heritage Books, 2007.

BY THE SAME AUTHOR

Genderstanding Jesus: Women in His View

In a world that increasingly holds religion responsible for gender inequality, *Genderstanding Jesus* asks a thought-provoking question: "What would Jesus do about gender relations?"

Genderstanding Jesus examines the lives of women in the Bible through His eyes to reveal how Jesus directly addressed their subjugation and suffering. It documents Jesus' tendency to break with tradition to exonerate, liberate, and empower women.

Read and be challenged to do as Jesus did!

Genderstanding Leadership: Power to the Pew

Is there a gender gap between Christian ideology and practice? *Genderstanding Leadership* points out pervasive biblical misinterpretations that form the basis for a troubling link between religion and gender-based inequality and even violence.

Genderstanding Leadership warns that the plight of women in the world will be directly affected by the treatment of women in the church.

Be inspired to take spirit-filled, strategic action for improved gender equality in religious institutions.

We invite you to view the complete
selection of titles we publish at:
www.TEACHServices.com

We encourage you to write us
with your thoughts about this,
or any other book we publish at:
info@TEACHServices.com

TEACH Services' titles may be purchased in
bulk quantities for educational, fund-raising,
business, or promotional use.
bulksales@TEACHServices.com

Finally, if you are interested in seeing
your own book in print, please contact us at:
publishing@TEACHServices.com

We are happy to review your manuscript at no charge.

www.ingramcontent.com/pod-product-compliance
Lightning Source LLC
Chambersburg PA
CBHW071214160426
43196CB00012B/2302